Talking to God

Portrait of a World at Prayer

foreword by Huston Smith

introduction by Phyllis Tickle

text by Karen Armstrong   The Dalai Lama   Mohandas K. Gandhi
Thich Nhat Hanh   Jack Kornfield   Harold Kushner   C. S. Lewis   Thomas Merton
Thomas Moore   Seyyed Hossein Nasr   Kathleen Norris   Pope John Paul II
David Steindl-Rast   Desmond Tutu   Elie Wiesel   Michael Wolfe   Carol Zaleski

edited by John Gattuso

Stone Creek Publications
Milford, New Jersey

FOR CARLA, GIOVANNA, REINA, AND NATALIA—ANGELS ALL.

Stone Creek Publications
460 Shire Road
Milford, NJ 08848
tel: 908-995-0016
screek@ptd.net
www.stonecreekpublications.com

Library of Congress Control Number: 2006925176
ISBN-13: 978-0-9656338-3-3
ISBN-10: 0-9656338-3-7

Distributed to the book trade by Independent Publishers Group
Printed in South Korea
Design Consultant: Rickabaugh Design

RIGHT: FOLLOWERS OF CAO DAI, WHICH DRAWS UPON ELEMENTS OF EASTERN AND WESTERN FAITHS, ATTEND A SERVICE AT THE GREAT TEMPLE IN TAY NINH, VIETNAM. PRECEDING PAGE: CHILDREN IN AMRITSAR, INDIA, PRAY AT SRI HARMANDIR SAHIB (THE GOLDEN TEMPLE), HOLIEST SHRINE OF THE SIKH RELIGION.

Contents

PRAYER FLAGS WAVE IN THE MOUNTAIN WINDS
OF LEH GOMPA, A SEVENTEENTH-CENTURY
BUDDHIST MONASTERY IN LADAKH, INDIA.

"*Don't pray when it rains if you don't pray when the sun shines.*"

Satchel Paige

LEFT: AN ARKANSAS BASEBALL TEAM
HUDDLES FOR A PRE-GAME PRAYER.
PRECEDING PAGES: NUNS AT THE CONVENT
OF THE SACRED HEART OF JESUS IN
MARSEILLE, FRANCE.

Prayer is often described as talking to God. That's the name of this book, and it's a useful way to think about prayer. But it's only a beginning. As you will discover in these pages, prayer is not limited to "talking" nor is it directed solely to a personal divinity, be it God, Allah, Yahweh, or one of the thousands of saints, prophets, avatars, bodhisattvas, or spirits recognized by the world's religions.

Words are important, of course, but words alone are not enough. In the Jewish tradition, for example, prayer is thought to be wholly genuine only when it is said with a heartfelt desire to communicate with the divine. The Hebrew word for this intention is *kavanah*. It is the presence of *kavanah* that makes the difference between merely saying prayers—that is, mouthing the words without any real meaning or understanding—and truly praying. Mahatma Gandhi, reflecting on the centrality of prayer in spiritual life, expressed a similar idea: "It is better in prayer to have a heart without words than words without a heart."

In some cases, prayer doesn't involve words at all. The most prayerful moments, the moments when you feel most attuned to the divine, can arrive in a variety of forms—in the singing of hymns, for instance, or the trancelike dances of Sufi dervishes. They can come in meditation or during periods of intense concentration, when the chattering mind is quiet and the ego still. They can come during an experience of nature, like Zen poets whose depiction of ordinary natural events—a jumping frog, a singing cuckoo, a shaft of moonlight—hint at the presence of a transcendent reality behind the veil of the physical world. Or they can come when you least expect them, when you are absorbed in work, or playing with your kids, or doing some mundane household chore. As Benedictine brother David Steindl-Rast points out, some people have their most authentic experience of prayer precisely when they are not saying prayers.

If such prayerful moments are available at any time, then maybe St. Paul's well-known admonition to "pray without ceasing" isn't quite as daunting as it may seem. There are those who have endeavored to do exactly as St. Paul instructs—devotees of the Jesus Prayer, for example, who train their minds to repeat the phrase "Lord Jesus Christ, have mercy on me" in every waking and even sleeping moment.

EVANGELICAL
CHRISTIANS AT
A PRAYER SERVICE
IN PHILADELPHIA,
PENNSYLVANIA.

But is there another understanding of Paul? Is it possible for prayer to pervade every aspect of our existence, to eat, sleep, work, and be with our families and neighbors as if doing these things were prayers themselves. In short, to live prayerfully, or as Buddhists might say, to live mindfully—fully aware of the sacredness of daily life, the miracle of every breath. These are things we usually become aware of only when some calamity shakes us out of our normal routine. Maybe that's what prayer does best; it wakes us up to the divine spark that resides in the here and now.

Prayer also has a petitionary quality, and this is perhaps its most familiar form. We don't simply talk to God, we ask for things. Even those of us who find prayer difficult or who practice no particular faith will occasionally send such a request heavenward. Who hasn't uttered a silent plea for help when events have slipped beyond our control, whether it be for something relatively prosaic—"Please, God, help the Red Sox win the pennant"—or something that shakes us right down to the core—"ease my child's pain ... let my father die peacefully ... make me worthy of my family's love"?

There are those who argue that this is prayer at its most selfish and unsophisticated, and, admittedly, it's not difficult to see how petitionary prayer can degenerate into a catalog of wishes, as if God could be cajoled or flattered into giving us what we want. And yet, even in the most self-serving petition there is a kernel of humility that resides at the very heart of prayer and maybe all religion. It is a frank recognition that despite all our wondrous ability to do great and sometimes terrible things in the world, we are still frightened, anxious, defensive, and achingly distant from our better selves. Ironically, scientists are among the first to recognize these limitations. "Not only is the universe stranger than we imagine," said astrophysicist Arthur Eddington, "it is stranger than we can imagine." The world's great mystics have been telling us the same thing for millennia: rational thought will only get us so far.

Are we to understand, then, that prayer is a method of influencing events that are otherwise beyond our control, a way to convince God to tip the scales in our direction? The answer, say the writers in this book, is an emphatic "no." As C. S. Lewis points out, prayer shouldn't be confused with magic, a kind of "infallible gimmick" to win God's favor. He reminds us that even Jesus's anguished prayer in the Garden of Gethsemane to "take this cup from me" was not granted. This is not to say that prayer is pointless or that it doesn't work, only that it works *on* us rather than *for* us.

Perhaps the most significant work that prayer does is to help us recognize the humanity of other people and deepen our capacity for compassion and forgiveness. As we come to terms with our own limitations and our own need for kindness and understanding, we see more clearly the same needs in others. Religious teachings may differ, but in the end we all live, suffer, and die in much the same way, and we pray for the same things—peace, health, patience, forgiveness.

It is often said that every religion embodies truth in its own way. That's an admirable thought, and, I think, essentially correct. But I wonder if it's equally instructive to argue that all religions are also inherently flawed, not because one is better or truer than another but because no system of human thought can fully reflect the sacred. Maybe, after 50,000 years of trying, we humans still don't have it exactly right. And maybe that's not such a bad thing. We have prayer to comfort us and the one rule that every great religion teaches: Treat others as you would have them treat you.

This same spirit of humility and compassion runs like a thread through every essay in this volume. You will find no definitive answers here, no easy prescriptions, no pat advice. What you will find are writers—many counted among the modern world's great spiritual thinkers—who have plunged deeply into the mystery of prayer and illuminated this most beautiful and elemental aspect of faith.

HINDU WOMEN GATHER FOR A FESTIVAL NEAR COLOMBO, SRI LANKA.

Foreword .... Huston Smith

This admirable book covers its subject so well that I had a hard time figuring out what I might add in this foreword. I finally decided that all of its chapters can be seen as icons." *Nice* Icons are inspired paintings that we look through like a window to behold the Ultimate Reality that is God. All of God's attributes converge, for there is no multiplicity in God. Still, we have to break his "singularity" into attributes, and my favorite is *Real.* God is the only completely Real thing there is—everything else is, in varying degrees, only partly real. When we human beings fail to live up to—fail to *real*-ize—the Spirit God breathed into us, we are to that degree unreal or, as I like to say, phony. When we pray, therefore, we are working to get rid of the phoniness in our lives. Sincere prayer is not always easy; it can be like cleansing our hearts with steel wool. When we pray sincerely, earnestly, and honestly, however, a window opens onto what we would like to be and might become. I found that iconic element in every entry in this book.

Icons inspire us, but they are not the totally Real to which they point. This limitation is rescued by Augustine's famous definition of God as a circle whose center is everywhere and circumference nowhere. That center is a point, actually a mathematical point because it occupies zero space, for God is not subject to the space and time that measure the universe God created. But that spaceless point opens out onto Augustine's circumference which is everywhere. Augustine tells us that when we pray we enter our centers where we are least phony and deepen that center. At the same time, prayer works like a springboard and propels us to move toward the circumference. In this way prayer exalts us. "Lift up your hearts," the liturgist intones, and the congregation responds, "We lift them up unto the Lord."

What a strange and wondrous fellowship the God-seekers in this book are, how rich the chorus of their prayers. While remaining true to our own faith, we should listen to these other voices, for by listening we may come to understand our fellowman, and understanding leads to love—a concept hallowed in every faith.

There is another gain in exploring prayer. Every act of worship incarnates some yearning in our own hearts; each altar is laid, each offering is shaped by hopes and fears that crouch in some corner of our own psyches. In this human sense the world's religions, however distant in miles and creed, are all "closer than breathing, nearer than hands and feet." As they lead the mind's eye outward they bend the soul's eye—the Third Eye as Tibetans call it—inward. In seeking to understand prayer in world faiths, we explore not only our world but our deepest selves.

Augustine

A JAPANESE GIRL ATTENDS MASS AT TOKYO CATHEDRAL.

Introduction .... Phyllis Tickle

Every body needs a lover; so does every soul. In their lovemaking, our bodies connect themselves to the natural order of which they each are a piece and part, producing the ongoing and sustaining stuff of that order and thereby working toward—indeed assuring—both its continuation as an order and its ever-restless variety and diversity. We in this country call that miracle of connection by the name of intercourse, a choice of labeling so exquisite that one must stop occasionally to honor its sheer, naked appropriateness.

Out of a kind of spiritual shyness, we call the lovemaking of the soul by the more staid, far less descriptive name of prayer, the delicious irony of the situation being that when pressed to define prayer, the scholars and theologians among us usually speak of it as "the intercourse of humanity with the divine." I suspect the more defensible way to arrive at a definition would be to assert from the beginning that prayer is lovemaking, to declare from the outset that prayer is intercourse between the soul and its natural order; for it is by prayer that the soul makes connection, assures the ongoing processes of the natural order of which it is a piece and part, and introduces the infinite variety and diversity which are the consummate celebrations of divine beauty.

All the records of humanity's experience within time, whether those records be visual or verbal or aural, are laced with images of, and testimonies to, the ecstatic and recurring fusion of both our bodies and our souls with that which is external to mundane perception. Almost always, too, those records of holy transport bear the cachet of an eroticism that limns the familiar beauty of what is being recorded. This book that you are holding, as you clearly can see for yourself, catches the faces and postures of thousands of us at prayer, and then augments those images with the commentary and insights of some of our most trusted and credible religion diarists. This is good, and that alone would make this volume a generous tool for private instruction. But I would submit that there is more here to which we need to turn our spirits' attention, if we want to arrive at the kind of richer vitalism this collection suggests.

All people pray. One certainly does not have to be either a deist or a theist in order to do that; one has only to answer the irresistible, keening cry of the soul for contact with its own kind. We err, in other words, when we think that all prayer goes "heavenward," however we

"Prayer…brings together two lovers, God and the soul."
Mechthild of Magdeburg

ABOVE: HANDS RAISED HEAVENWARD, A
CONGREGANT PRAYS DURING COMMUNION
AT IMAGO DEI COMMUNITY CHURCH IN
PORTLAND, OREGON.
OPPOSITE: A VILLAGER IN GUINEA-BISSAU
PERFORMS SALAT, A MUSLIM RITUAL PRAYER.

may, from within our various traditions, define that direction or location. To the contrary, prayer often is a kind of horizontal communion or intercourse of the soul with other souls who have known, do know, and will come to know experience within time. Prayer can be, and often is, the exposure of the soul's deficiencies or the spirit's errors to the correction of That Which Is. It can be an act of consummate joy that lifts the spirit as it overflows with amazement at its own sheer existence. Contrarily, of course, prayer can be a cry of abject rebellion and need, a kind of reaching out as well as up, to wrestle with the way things are. Prayer is, in other words, an activity which, whether private or corporate, is as varied in its possibilities as any other form of lovemaking; but prayer is also a place as surely as erotic transport is a place. Our artists and writers and singers have all been right about that.

Prayer is a describing strand within a non-locative terrain. It is a gathering place as unique in its construction as the souls who move in and out of it. It is a private bower where sweet intercourse occurs, but where agony and error can also be ripped out and laid bare for corrective surgery. It is home and yet occupies that no-place location which is itself only halfway home. It is to its realm of reference as the boudoir and the temple and the kitchen are in their realm to the body's reference; and the spirit knows both those referents well, being, as it is, unceasingly about the business of integrating the two of them into coherence.

Because I am writing about prayer in the opening decade of the twenty-first century, I am acutely aware that what I say here will come, long before the end of this century, to seem almost naive, if not outright antique, for we are already in the first stages of vast new understandings about human consciousness, about the place of the brain in temporal creation, the unbreakable union between body and soul, and the function of mind and its relation to will. All of these things are inextricably bound up with prayer as an action of more or less universal human conduct.

When, for instance, one speaks today of the efficacy of petitionary prayer, one assumes either the intervening

of the divine miraculous or of Einstein's inexplicable and mysterious "spooky." Within the next few decades, unless I and a lot of good folk smarter than I are very wrong, we will be able to show the mechanism by which the electricity-generating brain can and does manipulate and affect the structure of reality, both human and otherwise. That in itself will sharpen not only our understanding of what we do when we pray, but will also—and more significantly—allow us to separate out that which is entirely explicable by natural law from that which is not, to sift the predicated, in other words, from that which is indeed miraculous or, if you still prefer it, the spooky. Such is a consummation devoutly to be desired.

As an observant and totally persuaded Christian, I acknowledge with all my fellow-Abrahamics (as well as those of several other traditions) the existence of many gods of whom and over whom there is but One God Who Alone is God. I believe that the one God has entered time, making a rift in its containing and obscuring curtain, and holding open a way for me to pass, body and soul, through to that Eternal City which the present creation is in the business of populating. I acknowledge as well that in prayer we all celebrate as a common experience the miracle of our being here at all, given our great finitude, just as we exercise our spirits in raising up paeans of thankful praise in offering to the Glory and to the Giver of being.

"*Faith itself is the soul's true country, and prayer is its native language.*"
Donald Spoto

For me, as for any believer in the personed Divine, prayer is something more, however. It is, in other words, all these things, be they horizontal or vertical or simply skewed at some angle in between. Prayer is the place in which I read—in effect, am tutored in—the divine intent. It is the place where I meet, submit to, and am sculpted by God in preparation for my soul to assume its tiny and appointed place in the City of God. In addition, as a Christian, I understand—am told in my scripture—that what I ask for in and through the sacred name will be granted, which pledge, like all good promises, cuts two ways. It constitutes responsibility as much as privilege.

I said a moment ago that this singular book offers a great gift for our spirits' instruction. It does. By capturing, especially in its pictures, the universality of our prayers and of us as praying creatures, this book furnishes us with the road-ready beginnings of a new and better map into prayer, a better and far more useful traveler's guide to the place that is human prayer. It furnishes us, in effect, aerial photos of the common ground on which we know we meet when we pray, as well as a set of specifics by which to begin to draw up and map out the particulars of what each of our traditions teaches us about prayer.

I am a far better—far more intentional—Christian pray-er for having struggled with this book and its contents. Some other readers, pray God, will become more efficacious Buddhists or more observant Hindus or more devout Muslims. For what this book, in the end, persuasively offers us is the raw materials with which to begin to realize that while we may see different ends beyond the place that is prayer, we right now all come and go, to, from, and within, the same place. And when we who pray can meet there with unmediated recognition as well as with genuine awe that any of us is even there at all, we have begun to arrive at a new level of spiritual community. Then we will indeed be better able than ever before to assume our ability to shape this shared time of creation in accord with our expanding understanding of what prayer is to us as creatures as well as believers in varying gods.

So, I say again, let us all read and look at these pages, first to our own private benefit and, then, to that of our spirits' lives together.

Every Breath a Prayer

MORE THAN WORDS, PRAYER IS A STATE OF COMMUNION WITH THE DIVINE

Creating Faith .... Karen Armstrong

We tend to equate faith with believing certain things about God or the sacred. A religious person is often called a "believer" and as one who has adopted the correct ideas about the divine. Belief is thus seen as the first and essential step of the spiritual journey. Before we embark on a religious life, which must make considerable demands on our moral, social, professional, and personal affairs, we think that we must first satisfy ourselves intellectually that there is a God or that the truths of our particular tradition—Jewish, Christian, Muslim, Buddhist, Hindu, or whatever—are valid. It seems pointless to make a commitment unless we are convinced about the essentials. In our modern, scientific world, this makes good, rational sense: First you establish a principle, and then you apply it.

But the history of religion makes it clear that this is not how it works. To expect to have faith before embarking on the disciplines of the spiritual life is like putting the cart before the horse. In all the great traditions, prophets, sages, and mystics spend very little time telling their disciples what they ought to believe. Indeed, it is only since the Enlightenment that faith has been defined as intellectual submission to a creed. Hitherto, faith had been seen as a virtue rather than a prerequisite. It meant trust, and was used in rather the same way as when we say that we have faith in a person or an ideal. Faith was thus a carefully cultivated conviction that, despite all the tragic and dispiriting evidence to the contrary, our lives did have some ultimate meaning and value. You could not possibly arrive at faith in this sense before you had lived a religious life. Faith was thus the fruit of spirituality, not something that you had to have at the start of your quest.

All the great teachers of spirituality in all the major traditions have, therefore, insisted that before you can have faith, you must live in a certain way. You must lead a compassionate life, transcending the demands of the clamorous ego and recognizing the sacred in others; you must perform rituals (often enshrined in religious law) that make even the most mundane detail of our lives an encounter with the ultimate; all traditions insist that you must also pray. Prayer is thus not born of belief and intellectual conviction; it is a practice that creates faith.

This remarkable anthology shows the universality of prayer. Hindus, Buddhists, Native

Americans, African tribespeople, Jews, Christians, and Muslims all have very different beliefs, yet when they address the sacred, they do so in strikingly similar ways. It is surprising that prayer is such a universal practice, since it is fraught with problems. Everybody insists that the ultimate and the transcendent—called variously God, Nirvana, Brahman, or the sacred—cannot be defined in words or concepts, and yet, as these pages show, men and women habitually attempt to speak to the divine. Why do they do this, and what are the implications of this verbal attempt to bridge the yawning gulf that separates us from the sacred? Many Hindus, for example, see Brahman as strictly impersonal: It cannot, therefore, be addressed as "Thou"; it cannot speak to human beings nor relate to them in a personal way; it cannot "love" or get "angry." But at the same time, Brahman sustains and pervades us. It is so bound up with our very existence that it is not really appropriate to speak to it or think about it, as though it were a separate entity. And yet, as this volume shows, Hindus pray like the rest of us. They thank, they beseech, they crave forgiveness. Why?

Prayer, one might think, should be easier for Jews, Christians, and Muslims, since their God is experienced as a personal being. As the Bible and the Koran show, he can get angry and feel love for us; he can speak to us and encounter us. Even so, there are difficulties. Does God really need to be told by us that he created the world and redeemed us and that we are miserable sinners? Surely he knows all this already. Does he demand that we thank him, praise him, and plead for mercy? There is something slightly repellent in this notion, as it suggests a despotic deity who demands endless sycophantic obeisance from his worshipers. And what does it mean to refer, as I have just done, to God as "he"? Theologians constantly remind us that God goes beyond all human categories, including that of gender. Yet it is so difficult to avoid gender words—to say nothing of the limiting and even abhorrent ways in which such qualities as "anger," "love," and the like suggest a God who is all too human. All talk of and to God stumbles under great difficulties. Is there not a danger that our prayers will anthropomorphize God, making "him" loom in our imaginations as being like ourselves only writ large, with feelings, intentions, and inadequacies similar to our own? If we are not careful, our prayers can cut God down to size and help us to create a deity in our own images and likenesses. Such a God can only be an idol and hence offensive to the true spirit of monotheism.

The prayers in this book show that when men and women pray, they are in some profound sense talking to themselves. This does not mean that they are not also addressing the ultimate, since all the world's faiths do not see the sacred as simply Something "out there" but as a Reality that is also encountered in the depths of our own beings. But it is also true that people who pray are addressing deep personal needs and fears. We live in a frightening world and are the prey of mortality, injustice, cruelty, disaster, and an evil that can seem palpable and overwhelming. Unlike other animals, we humans fall very easily into despair. The prayers in this volume show that from a very early date, people have made themselves confront their terrors. They have invoked them, described them to themselves in prayer (as well as in art—a related activity), and in so doing have managed to reach beyond them. Men and women have always sensed that there is, in spite of the horrors that flesh is heir to, "an ultimate rightness of things," a Beneficence that is not only outside them but within. Prayers, such as that of Saint Patrick, attempt to invoke that benign power and strength that will enable us finally to lighten the darkness in the depths of the self.

We rarely allow ourselves to voice these deep fears

"Prayer is simply talking to God,
He speaks to us: we listen. We speak to him: he listens."

Mother Teresa

An offering of incense and flowers is left at the feet of a Hindu idol in the village of Ubud, Bali.

and anxieties. We are all struggling to survive. We cannot afford to admit our weakness and terror too freely. We are fearful of burdening others; we do not want to appear weak or open ourselves to exploitation in the battle that is life. We protect ourselves in all kinds of ways, especially by means of words. We are cautious and defensive and use language to bolster our sense of self for our own sakes as well as to impress others. We are rarely willing to admit our shortcomings and are quick to respond to a slight with a verbal counteroffensive. We make jokes to ward off our sense of life's tragedy or to make others (whom we fear or envy) objects of ridicule. We have fits of meanness in which we feel impaired by others' success. We exalt our own achievements, scuttle over our humiliations, shield ourselves from hurt, and make derogatory remarks about those who threaten our sense of security in ways that we do not always understand. We thus turn our words into weapons that attack as well as defend. All such activity embeds us in the prison of our own frightened egos.

Prayer helps us to liberate ourselves and to use language in an entirely different way, as these pages show. In prayer, we learn to acknowledge our vulnerability, our frailty, our failures, and our sins. By putting our unutterable weaknesses into words, we make them more real to ourselves but also make them more manageable. When we admit that we need forgiveness, we realize in a new way that this will be impossible unless we also forgive. We

give voice to our neediness, our longing, our terror. This daily discipline helps us to break through the defensive carapaces that we all form around ourselves, thus allowing the Benevolence and Rightness for which we long to penetrate the prisons of our cautionary being.

This process can be discerned in nearly every section of this book but especially in the prayers of the mystics. These geniuses of spirituality have learned the difficult art of opening themselves to something greater. They speak of the importance of ridding ourselves of negativity and defensiveness; of accepting the realities of suffering and imperfection; and of becoming aware of our longing for Something that transcends the pettiness and anxiety of our self-bound existence. Mystics also praise the virtue of voluntary poverty, which divests the self of the possessiveness that can only impede our progress. They speak of a Wisdom that is not an achievement of our own, to be used to advance our egotism and to help us to exploit the world and others for our own benefit; this wisdom is instead seen as a gift and attribute of the divine.

But prayer is not only an expression of fragility. Human beings have always experienced the world with awe and wonder. Despite the terrors and sorrows of the cosmos, its grandeur and beauty fill us with delight. It seems that the more we learn about the world, the more this sense of wonder increases. We used to think that science would eliminate this and make the mystery of the universe plain. But this has not happened. Sometimes, cosmologists and physicists today appear to be creating a new type of religious discourse, making us confront the dark world of uncreated reality as the mystics did and forcing us to see that the nature of existence exceeds the narrow compass of our minds. Thus, science, which can impart a false sense of pride and self-sufficiency, can also impart a humbling experience of our ignorance, smallness, and limitations. It can lead us to that attitude of silent awe of which the great contemplatives speak.

Yet the sheer busy-ness of our lives often leaves little time for contemplation. The world can become familiar to us. The prayers of praise and thanksgiving in this volume help to correct this. When they list the wonders of creation, these prayers are not groveling attempts to flatter the Creator but serve to remind us of the marvels that exist all around us. They thus help us to see what is really there: a mystery that cannot be simplistically defined but that becomes apparent when we learn how to strip away the veil of familiarity that obscures it. Such prayers help to hold us in the attitude of wonder that is characteristic of the best religion. Other prayers help us to put ourselves in tune with the fundamental laws of existence, to submit ourselves to the rhythms of the seasons and the cosmos. By cultivating a sense of these great laws and truths, our own egotistical concerns are put into perspective. By learning to see the sacred in the world around us, we will approach it with reverence. The world becomes what Muslims call an *ayah* (a sign) of God, not something to be exploited or greedily ran-

sacked for our gain. Finally, such prayers of thanksgiving help us to cultivate that sense of gratitude that is so often difficult to achieve in our daily battle for survival. When we feel insecure, it is sometimes hard to express the debt we owe to others for our achievements. By making us list the benefits we have received and give voice to our thanks, prayer helps us to acquire a warm, inner sense of favors received. Instead of feeling hard done by, we learn that we are perhaps more fortunate than we know.

Prayers thus create an attitude from which true faith and conviction can grow. But they are never ends in themselves: Most traditions have taught men and women to go beyond words into the Silence beyond through the repetition of a mantra...These teach us that our words cannot define God or the divine mystery, no matter how eloquent our prayer. They can serve only as springboards to the sacred, helping us to open ourselves to the deeper currents of existence and thus to live more intensely and fully.

But prayer cannot be effective unless it is accompanied by the ethical practices of religion, particularly by the virtue of compassion, which, all the major religions insist, is the one and only test of true spirituality. All too often, however, religious people can fall into the trap of self-righteousness and intolerance. Some find it impossible to believe that other traditions are valid paths to the divine. This book should help to correct such a tendency. By learning to pray the prayers of people who do not share our beliefs, we can learn at a level deeper than the cerebral to value their faith.

IRANIAN WOMEN GATHER FOR PRAYERS TO CELEBRATE THE END OF RAMADAN, A MONTH OF FASTING.

"The fewer the words, the better the prayer."

Martin Luther

BUDDHISTS GATHER AT A PAGODA IN PINDAYA CAVE NEAR THE LAKESIDE VILLAGE OF PINDAYA IN MYANMAR. USED FOR CENTURIES AS A PLACE OF MEDITATION AND WORSHIP, THE CAVERNS SHELTER THOUSANDS OF BUDDHA IMAGES AND STATUES.

ELEMENTARY SCHOOL STUDENTS IN LEH,
INDIA, ASSEMBLE FOR MORNING PRAYER.

Lord, make me an instrument of your peace.

Where there is hatred, let me sow love,

Where there is injury, pardon,

Where there is doubt, faith,

Where there is despair, hope,

Where there is darkness, light,

Where there is sadness, joy.

O Divine Master, grant that I may not so much

seek to be consoled as to console,

not so much to be understood as to understand,

not so much to be loved, as to love;

for it is in giving that we receive,

it is in pardoning that we are pardoned,

it is in dying that we awake to eternal life.

—*St. Francis of Assisi*

An Instinct for Prayer .... Thomas Moore

Human beings have a natural impulse to pray. One of my favorite forms is to sing or recite the psalms of the Bible: "Like the deer that yearns for running streams, so my soul yearns for you, O God." When I was young and chanted these words every day, they didn't penetrate very far into me. But today, closer to the end, tenderly tied to my children, aware of the need to turn from self to the unnamed God, the psalms give my words sentiments that I could not find on my own.

The obvious reason to pray is from need, but we also turn to prayer in thanks, praise, blessing, and remembrance. Prayer doesn't require belief in a personal God but may be an expression of absolute dependency and an appreciation for the mysteries. Prayer requires being in dialogue with life, having at least a vague sense of the other who defines us.

Of course we labor under the illusion that only humans can and should talk to each other. To the scientific eye the world doesn't have personality. We have looked into molecules and atoms and neutrons and have seen only empty space. There is no one there. No one to pray to. No one to listen to our prayer. To pray, many conclude, is to talk to yourself or to stand in front of the mirror of your projections.

But this is only one myth about the way things are. We see what our imaginations allow us to see, and we are always looking through the filter of a myth that we take as true and obvious. The microscope is an extension not only of the eye but also of the myth through which the eye sees. If we can't imagine God, we will not see any signs of divinity.

But it is possible to see differently, to reject the scientific myth as the only possible screen for experience. Opening up the pores of sensation—or the doors of perception, as Blake called them—we might sense more in the world than can be seen with the literal eye. We might perceive the world's beauty, its presence as a whole and in parts in relation to us, and our family relationship to it. We might sense a stirring there, a spark—scintilla, the ancients called it. We might sense, as Meister Eckhart said, an eye looking back at us as we look into the world.

One day many years ago my wife came to me early in the morning to show me her home pregnancy test. I looked closely and saw the faintest mark indicating a positive result. It was

the first indication of my daughter's presence in the world and in my life. That little mark felt momentous. Months later the doctor told me to look as she was being born. I saw red hair, only red hair, and she was not yet born. Another sign of her presence. Now I look at the pond at the bottom of our hill and at the fullness of life in that pond, and I think I glimpse a spark not entirely different from the signals of my daughter's arrival. I don't know what that spark is, that scintillating that is hardly perceptible. I can only imagine. But whatever it is, I can talk to it and come to it for consolation, just as I found "proof" of God's existence in the scintillating Galway inlet.

Prayer is foremost a way of being. Sometimes it finds its ways into words, but even when it doesn't, it makes life a dialogue. I don't know how other people are, but I am always talking inwardly to presences that I take as real—my dead grandparents, an animal, existence itself, or no one in particular. I find myself in the midst of that otherness, and I talk to it. I talk to the trees that are so tall and green and branching around the house. I'm in awe of the stones that stick up from the earth around us like hints of eternity in a world of change,

who withdrew into a closed room or a cloistered building for the sole purpose of praying.

Prayer makes us holy. It represents our awareness that we live in at least two universes: the world of the senses that we control—ego—and the world of mystery and timelessness that far transcends our abilities. By keeping these two universes connected, prayer makes holiness possible. Modern scholars talk about prayer as performance language. It doesn't merely express, it accomplishes something, and one of the things it accomplishes is holiness.

Prayer also helps hold families and communities together. The intention to be a family or a community is not enough. But the recognition, expressed in prayer, of a deeper source of connectedness is effective. People come together mysteriously. They may not know exactly what they're doing. Prayer acknowledges that mystery, and so appropriately we pray at weddings and funerals, before meals, and at gatherings. That is why lovemaking, too, is prayer.

In another context I've quoted the composer Monteverdi, saying that there are three passions: love, anger, and prayer. I prefer to think of prayer as a passion, as a way to take life on and respond to it as fully as possible. Prayer doesn't arise out of meekness and need only; it expresses our strength and is a sign of deep intelligence. We pray because we can stretch beyond our narcissism, knowing that our life is a grace and that the mysteries we are born into ask for acknowledgment.

The way we pray depends on how we imagine God. If we use the name of God, it is fairly easy to pray since we sense the personality of that which is beyond comprehension. If we don't use the name of God we can still pray from the awareness of a creator or simply a presence in the very marrow of life, a presence not clearly defined and yet still sufficiently other to allow dialogue.

Prayer can be subtle and sophisticated or plain and simple. I use many forms of prayer that come mainly

and I connect with them, as Jung did as a young man.

Many people today are trying to prove that prayer works. It is an attitude that I can't appreciate. What does it mean to work? Is prayer effective when we get what we want? Is prayer only petition and worth the effort if our prayers cause some change in the physical world? Are my wishes the measure of prayer's effectiveness?

I simply trust the impulse to pray. It is strong and sometimes overwhelming. Besides, people all over the world pray. It is clearly a natural instinct and therefore can be trusted as valuable. I can understand those mystics

CELEBRATION OF THE COPTIC MASS
IN GONDAR, ETHIOPIA.

from my childhood. My mother, who is an expert at prayer, taught me well, and I also learned much in the monastery. When an image comes to me of a friend or relative who has passed on, without thinking I say a Hail Mary. Whenever I hear an emergency siren, another Hail Mary. When my daughter was injured, I prayed so fast and hard I had no mind for anything else.

This approach to prayer may appear naïve, but life not fully explained has a basic simplicity about it. To be in touch with invisible presences need not be naïve; on the contrary it may represent a vital and sophisticated religious imagination. I don't have to know how prayer works or prove to myself or anybody else that there is someone or something on the other side of the dialogue. It is enough to sense the impulse to pray, to have some imagination of a holy other, and to act on that awareness in simple ways.

Religious traditions have created a vast culture of prayer—words, songs, gestures, objects, places, times, and formats. Prayer is the soul of religion because it comes from the heart and is often expressed beautifully, as in the words of the psalms: "I place all my trust in you, my God; all my hope is in your mercy." These simple words could transform a political party if they were seen for their subtlety and intelligence.

In Sophocles' *Oedipus* the chorus teaches Oedipus how to pray to the eumenides, the kindly gods of the earth. To these gods he should pray silently, they say, with no shouts or display. The prayer of the deep soul is appropriately quiet and reflective. It is inspired by deep feeling, and it makes sense to perform this prayer

more with reflection than with formality. Part of being a religious person is to know when and how to pray.

I was taught as a monk to pray without ceasing, to see every moment and every action as a prayer. I can see now that praying at all times takes us out of the relentless streaming of life and into eternity, and this is a good way to prepare for death, which, as a form of the eternal, is an aspect of living. If we don't pray, how can we be ready for death?

Prayer lies at the heart of Hindu tradition and is summarized beautifully in the words of Ramana Maharshi: "When you pray for God's grace, you are like someone standing neck-deep in water and yet crying for water. It is like saying that someone standing neck-deep in water feels thirsty, or that a fish in water feels thirsty, or that water feels thirsty." These powerful words remind us that from a holy imagination everything is grace, everything is godly, and therefore prayer is the most natural and available thing in the world. If we don't pray, it must be because we are inhibiting it in some way, for it will flow of its own accord.

In the library of our house, high above the door, we have painted a brief prayer from Nicholas of Cusa: *Ubicumque me verto ades*—Wherever I turn, you are there. This, to me, is a reminder of the omnipresence of God and the ubiquity of prayer. We need to be reminded, not to pray, but that we are praying.

Prayer connects me to the depths and heights of the world in which I live. If I don't pray, I live as though life were wafer thin and purely horizontal. But when I pray, I bring to bear the vertical dimensions, which

offer meaning and value. Everything that is done in the practical world is completed by prayer. All the effort finds its value in being tied to the mysteries.

Prayer is a means of breaking through the limitations of secular discourse and thought and of a too narrowly circumscribed world. Prayer is a kind of intellectual sacrifice in which we give up the illusion of self-reliance and extend our need for another to the very limit. It enlarges the sense of self and world, and makes connections between them.

Meister Eckhart describes prayer at its best as a sinking down into "God's dearest will," a lovely phrase which of course can be taken naïvely but might also be understood as the affectionate and benign source of our lives. I would say that prayer at its best requires from many of us that we give up all naïve notions of God, emptying ourselves of all intention and manipulation, all expectations and demands, and exposing ourselves to the absolute but affectionate emptiness.

At the same time I think we can come to prayer with a strong sense of need, and that is also an expression of the deep soul. It should be possible to do both: sink into God's dearest will and be full of the thoughts and emotions of our need. There is a difference between demanding that life unfold as we expect it and feeling the most

profound anxiety in the face of tragedy and danger. Like Job we beg for some understanding without demanding it, and like the psalmist we pray, *"De profundis clamavi ad te Domine*—Out of the depths I cry to you, O Lord."

I should think it obvious that prayer emerges naturally out of anxiety, fear, and depression. These extreme emotions don't weaken prayer at all; in fact they reveal the connection between our deepest turmoil and our highest yearnings for transcendence. What else satisfies the longing that rises up from despair and anxiety? Not the easy explanations and encouragements of psychology. Not the equally anxious attempts of friends to spur us on past our anxieties. Prayer acknowledges fear and takes us beyond it. What could be more elegant?

People of simple faith may never consider the importance of emptiness in religion and yet make it part of their faith. Some people don't question the theology with which they have grown up, and yet their faith matures over time into something approaching absolute. The prayer that rises out of this kind of faith is also powerful and not as naïve as might be supposed.

Nicholas of Cusa is an example of one who can be intellectually sophisticated and at the same time search for simple ways to be pious. "Whoever seeks God might remember that in God's name is contained a certain path for seeking God so that God can be groped for." The point in this intellectually honest approach to prayer is not to grasp but to grope. As in all matters of religion there is no final certainty and no final outcome. Through prayer we approach the mysteries, but we don't conquer them.

The mystic advises us to pray always, to simply be aware of the grace that permeates everything at every moment just as the water permeates the lake. There is nothing to do but stand in this water. Like fish we breathe in the life-giving nutrients that are naturally present. We understand that grace is not given apart from life but is food for the soul that saturates everything in existence.

RIGHT: PILGRIMS CONVERGE ON THE BRAZILIAN CITY OF CONGONHAS DO CAMPO FOR THE ANNUAL JUBILEU DO SENHOR BOM JESUS DO MATOSINHOS TO PRAY, DO PENANCE, AND RECEIVE BLESSINGS.
ABOVE: ZOROASTRIANS PRAY IN AN ANCIENT TEMPLE AT IRAN'S CHAKCHAK MOUNTAIN.

"The most powerful prayer...
is that which proceeds from
an empty spirit."

Meister Eckhart

HINDU HOLY MEN, OR SADHUS, GATHER AT
THE KUMBH MELA FESTIVAL IN ALLAHABAD,
INDIA. KUMBH MELA IS HELD ONCE EVERY
TWELVE YEARS AND IS THE LARGEST EVENT IN
THE HINDU CALENDAR, ATTRACTING MILLIONS
OF PILGRIMS TO THE BANKS OF THE GANGES
RIVER TO PRAY, MAKE OFFERINGS, AND BATHE
IN THE SACRED WATERS.

The Core of Life .... Mohandas K. Gandhi

I am glad that you all want me to speak to you on the meaning of and the necessity for prayer. I believe that prayer is the very soul and essence of religion, and, therefore, prayer must be the very core of the life of man, for no man can live without religion. There are some who in the egotism of their reason declare that they have nothing to do with religion. But it is like a man saying that he breathes but that he has no nose. Whether by reason, or by instinct, or by superstition, man acknowledges some sort of relationship with the divine. The rankest agnostic or atheist does acknowledge the need of a moral principle, and associates something good with its observance and something bad with its nonobservance. [Charles] Bradlaugh, whose atheism is well known, always insisted on proclaiming his innermost conviction. He had to suffer a lot for thus speaking the truth, but he delighted in it and said that truth is its own reward. Not that he was quite insensible to the joy resulting from the observance of truth. This joy, however, is not at all worldly, but springs out of communion with the divine. That is why I have said that even a man who disowns religion cannot and does not live without religion.

Now I come to the next thing, viz., that prayer is the very core of man's life, as it is the most vital part of religion. Prayer is either petitional or in its wider sense is inward communion. In either case the ultimate result is the same. Even when it is petitional, the petition should be for the cleansing and purification of the soul, for freeing it from the layers of ignorance and darkness that envelop it. He, therefore, who hungers for the awakening of the divine in him must fall back on prayer. But prayer is no mere exercise of words or of the ears, it is no mere repetition of empty formula. Any amount of repetition of Ramanama [God's name] is futile if it fails to stir the soul. It is better in prayer to have a heart without words than words without a heart. It must be in clear response to the spirit which hungers for it. And even as a hungry man relishes a hearty meal, a hungry soul will relish a heartfelt prayer. And I am giving you a bit of my experience and that of my companions when I say that he who has experienced the magic of prayer may do without food for days together but not a single moment without prayer. For without prayer there is no inward peace.

"He who is in the sun, and in the fire and in the heart of man is One. He who knows this is one with the One."

The Upanishads

ABOVE: A PARISHIONER LIGHTS VOTIVE CANDLES AT EL SANTUARIO DE CHIMAYO IN NEW MEXICO. THE SHRINE HOUSES A WELL OF SOIL CREDITED WITH MIRACULOUS HEALINGS.
FOLLOWING PAGES: JAVANESE MONKS COMMEMORATE THE BUDDHA'S BIRTH, ENLIGHTENMENT, AND PASSING AWAY AT A VESAK CEREMONY.

If that is the case, someone will say, we should be offering our prayers every minute of our lives. There is no doubt about it, but we, erring mortals, who find it difficult to retire within ourselves for inward communion even for a single moment, will find it impossible to remain perpetually in communion with the divine. We, therefore, fix some hours when we make a serious effort to throw off the attachments of the world for a while, we make a serious endeavor to remain, so to say, out of the flesh. You have heard Surdas' hymn. It is the passionate cry of a soul hungering for union with the divine. According to our standards he was a saint, but according to his own he was a proclaimed sinner. Spiritually he was miles ahead of us, but he felt the separation from the divine so keenly that he has uttered that anguished cry in loathing and despair.

I have talked of the necessity for prayer, and there-through I have dealt with the essence of prayer. We are born to serve our fellow man, and we cannot properly do so unless we are wide awake. There is an eternal struggle raging in man's breast between the powers of darkness and of light, and he who has not the sheet-anchor of prayer to rely upon will be a victim to the powers of darkness. The man of prayer will be at peace with himself and with the whole world. The man who goes about the affairs of the world without a prayerful heart will be miserable and will make the world also miserable. Apart therefore from its bearing on man's condition after death, prayer has incalculable value for man in this world of the living. Prayer is the only means of bringing about orderliness and peace and repose in our daily acts. We inmates of the ashram who came here in search of truth and for insistence on truth professed to believe in the efficacy of prayers, but had never up to now made it a matter of vital concern. We did not bestow on it the care we did on other matters. I woke from my slumbers one day and realized that I had been woefully negligent of my duty in the matter. I have, therefore, suggested measures of stern discipline and far from being any worse, I hope we are the better for it. For it is so obvious. Take care of the vital thing and other things will take care of themselves. Rectify one angle of a square, and the other angles will be automatically right.

Begin, therefore, your day with prayer, and make it so soulful that it may remain with you until the evening. Close the day with prayer so that you may have a peaceful night free from dreams and nightmares. Do not worry about the form of prayer. Let it be any form, it should be such as can put us into communion with the divine. Only, whatever be the form, let not the spirit wander while the words of prayer run on out of your mouth.

Prayers and Prayerfulness .... David Steindl-Rast

May we presume that everyone knows what prayer is? From one point of view the answer is "yes." Every human being knows prayer from experience. Have we not all experienced moments in which our thirsting heart found itself with surprise drinking at a fountain of meaning? Much of our life may be a wandering in desert lands, but we do find springs of water. If what is called "God" means in the language of experience the ultimate Source of Meaning, then those moments that quench the thirst of the heart are moments of prayer. They are moments when we communicate with God, and that is, after all, the essence of prayer.

But do we recognize these meaningful moments as prayer? Here, the answer is often "no." And under this aspect we cannot presume that everyone knows what prayer is. It happens that people who are in the habit of saying prayers at certain set times have their moments of genuine prayer precisely at times when they are not saying prayers. In fact, they may not even recognize their most prayerful moments as prayer. Others who never say formal prayers are nourished by moments of deep prayerfulness. Yet, they would be surprised to learn that they are praying at all.

Suppose, for example, you are reciting Psalms. If all goes well, this may be a truly prayerful experience. But all doesn't always go well. While reciting Psalms, you might experience nothing but a struggle against distractions. Half an hour later you are watering your African violets. Now, suddenly the prayerfulness that never came during the prayers overwhelms you. You come alive from within. Your heart expands and embraces those velvet leaves, those blossoms looking up to you. The watering and drinking become a give-and-take so intimate that you cannot separate your pouring of the water from the roots' receiving, the flower's giving of joy from your drinking it in. And in a rush of gratefulness your heart celebrates this belonging together. As long as this lasts, everything has meaning, everything makes sense. You are communicating with your full self, with all there is, with God. Which was the real prayer, the Psalms or the watering of your African violets?

Sooner or later we discover that prayers are not always prayer. That is a pity. But the other half of that insight is that prayer often happens without any prayers. And that should cheer

Worshipers pray at the Bhaktivedanta Manor Hare Krishna Temple in Aldenham, England, during the joyous Janmashtami Festival celebrating Krishna's birth.

us up. In fact, it is absolutely necessary to distinguish between prayer and prayers. At least if we want to do what Scripture tells us to do and "pray continually" (Lk 18:1) we must distinguish praying from saying prayers. Otherwise, to pray continually would mean saying prayers uninterruptedly day and night. We need hardly attempt this to realize that it would not get us very far. If, on the other hand, prayer is simply communication with God, it can go on continually. In peak moments of awareness this communication will be more intense, of course. At other times it will be low key. But there is no reason why we should not be able to communicate with God in and through everything we do or suffer and so "pray without ceasing" (1 Thess 5:17).

Maybe I shouldn't have mentioned uninterrupted prayer at all. The very thought may seem overawing and scare someone off. Many of us might, in fact, say: "Praying at all times? Goodness! From where I find myself it would be a long way even to praying at those times when I am saying my prayers!" All right, then, let us start once again where we are. What is it that makes our prayers truly prayer? If only we could somehow catch on to the secret of that spontaneous prayerfulness. That would be the clue to praying when we are saying prayers. Eventually it may even lead to praying at all times.

Those of us who have been saying prayers every day for many years and who have been trying to make our prayers truly prayer should have some answer to the question: What is it that makes prayers prayer? When we try to put into words what the secret might be, words like mindfulness, full alertness, and wholehearted attention suggest themselves. Those are, of course, the characteristics also of our spontaneous moments of prayer. The difference is that the wakefulness which comes spontaneously at those special moments often costs us an effort at times of formal prayer. The technical term for that effort and for the state of mind that results from it is, in the Catholic tradition, "recollection."

Most Catholic Christians know what recollection means. At least they are familiar with the term. Others might associate recollection with memories. As a technical term, however, recollection means a special kind of mindfulness in prayer, a mindfulness that is identical with prayerfulness. When I am fully recollected, my prayers are fully prayer. As I get more distracted, my prayers run dry. Finally, my prayers may be an empty formality. When recollection is scattered by distractions, prayers are merely the empty husk of prayer. If recollection is that important for our prayer life, it might be worthwhile to examine more closely what we mean by it, and how we can cultivate that special kind of prayerful mindfulness.

Mindfulness implies concentration. Concentration is, therefore, an essential ingredient of recollection in prayer. Those of us who have learned to concentrate on what we are doing are well on the way to recollection. And yet, no amount of concentration will, by itself, make us recollected. The reason is this: Concentration normally narrows down our field of attention. It makes all our attentiveness converge on one focal point and, in the process, tries to eliminate everything else from our field of vision. We could compare this process of concentration with focusing a large magnifying glass. At first a good portion of the page might appear within its frame, but blurred. As we bring one single word or letter clearly into focus, all else is eliminated from our view. In a similar sense, concentration normally implies elimination.

Now, recollection is that full kind of mindfulness which T. S. Eliot calls "concentration without elimination." This is, of course, a paradox. But shouldn't we expect a paradox here? Do not all opposites coincide in God? How then could we encounter God in prayer and not be struck by paradox?

But how can there be a concentration *without* elimination? Because concentration can remain itself and yet coincide with an altogether different attitude that makes it include all that concentration alone would tend to eliminate. Recollection has two ingredients.

Concentration is only one. The other one is what I call wonderment. For lack of a better term, wonderment stands here for a kind of sustained surprise. But our two ingredients of recollection do not mix easily. Wonderment and concentration seem to run counter to one another. While concentration tends to narrow down one field of vision, as we saw, wonderment is expansive. That these two movements coincide in recollection is just another expression of the paradox. Even the two bodily gestures associated with wonderment and concentration contradict one another. When we want to concentrate, we wince our eyes. We might think that this helps us focus our vision on something we want to look at with great concentration. But watch what happens when we want to concentrate intently on a faint or distant sound. We might also find ourselves wincing our eyes as we say, "I can barely make out what I'm hearing." Are we wincing our eyes so as to hear better? Well, we can't very well wince our ears, and yet our body wants to express the idea of eliminating everything except the one thing pinpointed for concentrated attention.

When you are filled with wonderment, however, your eyes are wide open. Just think of the eyes of a child in the zoo looking up to the elephants. Or think of your own eyes when you are standing under a starlit sky. You might even find yourself opening your arms wide as if your wide open eyes were not enough for your body to express your limitless openness.

Recollection combines this openness with concentration. How is my body to express this paradox? Am I going to wince one eye and open the other wide? I'm at a loss. But my heart can somehow deal with this paradox. That may be the reason why wholeheartedness comes closer to conveying the idea of recollection than mindfulness does. Paradox boggles the mind. But the heart thrives on paradox. We said that to speak of the heart is to speak of fullness. But only paradox can hold that fullness. The child in us understands this. For the child, too, thrives on paradox.

"God needs to hollow us out, to empty us in order to make room for himself."

Pierre Teilhard de Chardin

BUDDHISTS COME TO MEDITATE AND PRAY AT MYANMAR'S GOLDEN ROCK PAGODA, BUILT ATOP A GILDED BOULDER BALANCED PRECARIOUSLY ON THE EDGE OF A CLIFF.

ABOVE: ORTHODOX JEWS GATHER AT THE
WESTERN WALL IN JERUSALEM TO RECITE
PRAYERS AND READ SCRIPTURE.
FOLLOWING PAGES: ST. MAKARIOS
MONASTERY, WADI AL-NATRUN, EGYPT.

I found a master for myself, Moshe the Beadle.

He had noticed me one day at dusk, when I was praying.

"Why do you weep when you pray?" he asked me, as though he had known me a long time.

"I don't know why," I answered, greatly disturbed.

The question had never entered my head. I wept because—because of something inside me that felt the need for tears. That was all I knew.

"Why do you pray?" he asked me, after a moment.

Why did I pray? A strange question. Why did I live? Why did I breathe?

"I don't know why," I said, even more disturbed and ill at ease. "I don't know why."

After that day I saw him often. He explained to me with great insistence that every question possessed a power that did not lie in the answer.

"Man raises himself toward God by the questions he asks Him," he was fond of repeating. "That is the true dialogue. Man questions God and God answers. But we don't understand His answers. We can't understand them. Because they come from the depths of the soul, and they stay there until death. You will find the true answers, Eliezer, only within yourself!"

"And why do you pray, Moshe?" I asked him.

"I pray to the God within me that He will give me the strength to ask Him the right questions."

—*Elie Wiesel, from* Night

Praise and Supplication

DOES GOD RESPOND TO PRAYERS? DO WE UNDERSTAND THE ANSWERS?

Can Modern People Pray? .... Harold Kushner

Sister Rejeanne Kelley, A Roman Catholic nun, tells of the home in which she was raised: "My mother had a vigil light and a statue of St. Anthony. When she didn't get what she wanted, she would blow out the light and turn St. Anthony to the wall. When she got what she wanted, back he'd come and she'd light the candle again."

Some years ago, the papers carried the story of a man in Florida who sued his minister. It seems the man had been in church one Sunday when the minister gave a sermon based on the Scriptural passage "Cast thy bread upon the waters." He urged the congregation to be charitable and generous, telling them that God would reward them tenfold. The man subsequently made a large contribution to the church, and when his business did not prosper, sued the minister for false preaching. (The case was thrown out of court and the man was told to take sermons less literally. I wonder if the preacher argued in his own defense that giving money in order to be richly compensated was not charity but calculated investment.)

We tend to think that for religion to work, for our prayers to be answered, we should get what we ask for. That is to say, we have confused God with Santa Claus. We think that prayer means giving God the list of things we want and assuring Him that we have been good girls and boys and deserve to get them, and if we haven't been good, the rules we broke were silly rules anyway.

When we pray sincerely and intensely for something—the child praying to find a bicycle under the Christmas tree, the teenage girl praying for someone to find her attractive and love her, the adult praying for the survival and return to health of a loved one—when we shower God with pleas and promises and still don't get what we prayed for, we are left wondering what went wrong. Is there something wrong with us? Were our prayers not fervent enough, our promised changes not enough of a sacrifice? Are we not good enough people for God to heed our prayers?

Or is there something wrong with God, that He is not moved by our desperate plight and honest pleading? Why won't He give us what He seems so ready to give other, apparently less deserving people? Or maybe there is something wrong with religion itself. Maybe there is no God who hears prayers. Maybe our pouring out our hearts, our fears, our promises to change, end up in some celestial dead-letter office, "Addressee Unknown."

Sometimes the same thing happens when we attend church or synagogue, looking for a religious experience, looking for something spiritual to happen. Perhaps we are confused, perhaps we are spiritually hungry and lonely. We are not sure exactly what it is we are looking for, but we vaguely sense that the church or temple is the place to look for it, and that we will recognize it when we see it. An hour or two later, we walk out with the same feeling we have after seeing a mediocre movie. We find ourselves evaluating the sermon, the choir, the friendliness of the ushers, and deciding that all of them were well intentioned, but something, the one thing we went there looking for, was missing.

We wonder if the fault is in ourselves, that we never learned to appreciate religion any more than we learned to appreciate modern art. Are we perhaps spiritually tone-deaf? Or was it religion that is at fault? Perhaps it is a case of "the emperor's new clothes," where everyone really finds religion boring and irrelevant but is too polite or hypocritical to admit it.

I don't think any of these reactions is valid. There is nothing wrong with religion if we would only understand it properly, and neither is there anything so terrible about most of us that God should withhold from us the rewards of religion and prayer. What happens most of the time is that we are disappointed in religion because we are doing it wrong.

Too often, we try to use religion as a way of controlling and manipulating God. We think that if we say the right words or perform the right actions, we can get God to do what we want Him to. If we stopped to think about it, we might wonder how an awesomely powerful, all-wise God could be controlled by a few words from the likes of us. But after all, we might reason, a three-ton automobile can be made to do what we want with the pressure of our fingertips. The fearful power of electricity can be tamed to do our bidding. Computers are so much faster and more efficient at handling information than we are, but once we know how to operate them, we can make them do all sorts of things. And perhaps we remember how, when we were children, our parents were much more powerful than we were, but we mastered the art of persuading them to give us what we wanted from them because they loved us. So what is so unreasonable about attempting to control God?

Quite simply, God will not suffer Himself to be manipulated by our words or deeds. That is not religion. A century ago, Sir James Frazer, in *The Golden Bough,* suggested that this was the difference between religion and magic. Religion, he said, is the attempt to serve God. Magic is the effort to manipulate God. When we turn to religion as a way of getting God to give us what we want—be it health, love, riches, or whatever—we run the risk of being disappointed, not because we are unworthy of being loved or being rich, and not because God is stubborn or spiteful or incapable of helping us, but because that is not what religion does.

Prayer is not a matter of coming to God with our wish list and pleading with Him to give us what we ask

A PASSERBY PAUSES FOR A MOMENT
OF PRAYER OUTSIDE THE MONUMENTAL
TODAI TEMPLE IN NARA, JAPAN.

for. Prayer is first and foremost the experience of being in the presence of God. Whether or not we have our requests granted, whether or not we get anything to take home as a result of the encounter, we are changed by having come into the presence of God. A person who has spent an hour or two in the presence of God will be a different person for some time afterward.

I am told that the Eskimos have more than a dozen words for snow because snow is an important part of their environment. They find it useful to distinguish between falling snow, frozen snow, melted snow, and all its other forms. For us, snow is only an occasional inconvenience (I write these lines shortly after having shoveled it off the front walk of my Massachusetts home), so we make do with one word to cover all of its manifestations.

If prayer were an important part of our lives, instead of an occasional diversion, we would probably have many words for it. Instead, we stretch the same word to refer to a public reading of a prescribed liturgy at a prescribed time, to the desperate wish of a terminally ill woman, to the spontaneous gasp of delight and awe we feel when we see the sun on the mountain or the spring flowers or the stars on a clear night. Those are all prayers, those are all encounters with God, but they are very different spiritual experiences.

In congregational worship, regularly scheduled services on a Saturday or Sunday morning, I have come to believe that the congregating is more important than the words we speak. Something miraculous happens when people come together seeking the presence of God. The miracle is that we so often find it. Somehow the whole becomes more than the sum of its parts. A spirit is created in our midst which none of us brought there. In fact, each of us came there looking for it because we did not have it when we were alone. But in our coming together, we create the mood and the moment in which God is present.

The psalmist says, "Lord, I love Your Temple abode, the dwelling place of Your presence" [Psalm 26:8]. But an average Tuesday or Wednesday morning, the sanctuary of my synagogue stands dark and empty. I am not sure it can be described as "the dwelling place of [God's] presence." Only when people enter it in a mood of reverence and spiritual search does it become a house of worship.

We don't go to church or synagogue at a stipulated time because God keeps "office hours." We go because that is when we know there will be other people there, seeking the same kind of encounter we are seeking. That is why it makes sense to read words someone else has written, words that may or may not reflect what we believe. The purpose of reading those words is not to fool God into thinking we share the pious sentiments of the prayer's author. The purpose is for us to join in song and prayer with our fellow worshipers, to find God in the exhilarating experience of transcending our isolation, our individuality, and becoming part of a greater whole. When the service works, we will feel different about ourselves and the world for having gone through that experience.

But why does a congregational prayer service sometimes not work? Partly because miracles don't always happen when we schedule them, but partly too because even if the clergy and the choir and the ushers know their parts cold, we may not have learned ours. We go in thinking of ourselves as an audience, with the same anticipation we bring to a visit to the theater. "A good movie can reach me emotionally; let's see if a good religious service can do the same." (Sometimes the architecture of the house of prayer conspires to make us think that way. It invites us to sit back and watch the professionals perform.) But we can't be passive spectators if we want to experience the magic of worship. Without our active participation, it will not happen.

Sometimes services fall flat because we have lost the art of listening. We think prayer involves talking to God, persuading him, telling Him things He would not otherwise know. We may realize that millions of other people are bringing their cases before God, but we think that if we increase the intensity and fervor of our prayers, then, like the correspondent who shouts loudest at a White House press conference, our cry will catch God's ear. We need to be reminded that prayer involves listening perhaps even more than speaking. It involves opening ourselves to what God wants us to hear, in a setting purified of the noise and distractions of the everyday world.

When communication between a husband and wife breaks down so that they are no longer sharing with each other, the rift can take one of two forms. Either they can stop talking to each other entirely and sit walled off in silence, or they can fill the air between them with static, meaningless noise, verbal busywork, to hide the fact that they have nothing to say to each other. ("Please pass the vegetables." "What time do we have to pick up the kids?" "What's on television tonight?") When we lack the art of communicating with God, when we don't know how to talk to Him and don't know how to listen, we can show that either by keeping out of His way or by filling the channels with empty verbiage, pious-sounding words that never engage our hearts, as a way of trying to camouflage the fact that we don't know

ABOVE: HASSIDIC JEW, BROOKLYN, NEW YORK.
OPPOSITE: THE GNARLED HANDS OF AN ELDERLY PATIENT ARE BROUGHT TOGETHER IN PRAYER AT ST. ROSE'S HOSPICE IN NEW YORK CITY.

what to say to Him and don't believe He has anything to say to us.

If God is not Santa Claus and prayer is not primarily a matter of telling God what we would like Him to do to make us happy, what does prayer accomplish? For one thing, if we have learned to listen while we pray, prayer can remind us of things we would probably not be thinking of otherwise. Prayer can remind us to be grateful. Prayers of thanks for the food we eat remind us not to take it for granted. They serve not only to remind us of people going hungry, but of the miracle that occurs when seeds and soil, rain and sun combine to produce our daily sustenance. They remind us of the chain of people involved in producing, processing, packaging, and distributing the food that ends up on our tables.

The first five minutes of a Jewish daily morning service contain blessings in which I thank God for the fact that:

My mind works and I know it is morning,

My eyes work,

My arms and legs function,

My spinal column works and I can stand upright,

I have clothes to wear,

I have things to look forward to during the day.

Without these prescribed blessings, it might not occur to me to be grateful for all those things. I might have to wait until I encountered a blind man or a cripple, and then my gratitude would be mixed with a large dose of pity.

Gratitude does not come naturally to most people. We tend to assume that we are entitled to all the good things in life just for being the nice people we are. We have to be taught to be grateful. ("Say thank you to Grandpa for the present, and don't let him hear you complain that it's too small." "Did you write all the thank-you notes for your graduation presents?" "Honey, would you mind finishing writing the thank-you's for the wedding gifts? I find it a chore.")

There is a Hassidic story about the tailor who comes to his rabbi and says, "I have a problem with my prayers. If someone comes to me and says, 'Mendel, you're a wonderful tailor,' that makes me feel good. I feel appreciated. I can go on feeling good for a whole week, even longer, on the strength of one compliment like that. But if people came to me every day, one after another, hour after hour, and kept saying to me, 'Mendel, you're a wonderful tailor,' 'Mendel, you're a wonderful tailor,' over and over again, it would drive me crazy. It would soon get to the point where I wouldn't want to listen to them anymore. I would tell them to go away and let me do my work in peace. This is what bothers me about prayer. It seems to me that if we told God how wonderful He was once a week, even once every few weeks, and just one or two of us at a time, that's all He would need. Is God so insecure that He needs us praising Him every day? Three times a day, morning, noon, and night? Hundreds of people praising him? It seems to me it would drive Him crazy."

The rabbi smiled and said, "Mendel, you're absolutely right. You have no idea how hard it is for God to listen to all of our praises, hour after hour, day after day. But God knows how important it is for us to utter that praise, so in His great love for us, He tolerates all our prayers."

God does not need flattery, but we need to become the sort of people who know how to be grateful. Look at what we have done to Thanksgiving. We have made it a day on which we complain about having eaten too much, and then turn our attention to the football game, because we are so uncomfortable sustaining a sense of gratitude for more than a moment.

I once read an essay by a man who had formed the habit of writing "thank you" in the lower left-hand corner of all his checks as he paid his bills. He would write a check to the electric utility or the phone company, and as he penned in the words "thank you" in the corner, he would think of all the ways in which his life was made more comfortable by the fact that the company regularly and reliably provided him with its services. He would write a check to the bank for his monthly mortgage payment and pause for a moment to reflect on the comfort of having a roof over his head. He would pay his water bill and as he wrote "thank you" in the corner, he would say to himself that the water wasn't all that great-tasting and probably had some chemicals in it that were bad for him, but how long ago was it that his forebears had to pump water from the well in winter and worry about it going dry in summer. Even when he was not all that happy about writing a check, as when he paid his income tax in April, he disciplined himself to write "thank you" on the check, not because he believed that the IRS computer would notice it and be gratified, but because it was

his way of reminding himself that he should feel grateful to be living in this country and enjoying the benefits that American democracy provides.

Once we get over the Santa Claus mentality, prayer can be that kind of discipline, not an inventory of what we lack but a series of reminders of what we have, and what we might so easily take for granted and forget to be grateful for.

A man who has just been interviewed for a good job stops off at a church on the way home and prays that he gets the job. A woman visiting her husband in the coronary care unit of a hospital stops off at the hospital chapel to pray for his recovery. Do we really want to think of God as a God who has the power to grant those wishes, and chooses to give us or deny us what we pray for? Will praying affect either the employer's decision or the patient's recovery? Do we want to measure the usefulness of prayer on the basis of whether the man gets the job or not, whether the husband survives his heart attack or dies? I have religious friends who like to say, "God always answers our prayers, but sometimes the answer is no." I confess I don't like that outlook. It not only implies that God knows what is good for us better than we ourselves do, but that we should not weep or feel bad when things turn out wrong for us, because God wanted it to happen that way. That outlook leads us to believe that God could control everything for our benefit, that He could send us health and prosperity, if we could only find the right words and the right level of fervor to make Him want to.

Some people say God does not grant our prayers because people's prayers are mutually exclusive. Farmers pray for rain and families with picnics scheduled pray for sunshine. One group of fans prays for the home team to win, while another prays for the visitors. God can answer one set of prayers only by denying the other. I would rather believe rain is caused by meteorological factors,

ABOVE: A HINDU ENGINEER IN INDIA STRIKES A
DANCER'S POSE AS HE PRAYS TO THE RISING SUN.
HE POURS WATER TO HONOR THE GODDESS.
OPPOSITE: A BALINESE HINDU KNEELS TO
MAKE AN OFFERING OF INCENSE AND FLOWERS.

"Prayer is not asking. Prayer is putting oneself in the hands of God."
Mother Teresa

CHRISTIANS RAISE HANDS AND VOICES AT
A PRAYER MEETING IN DALLAS, TEXAS.

and that ball games are won by a combination of skill and luck, without God's intervening to arrange the outcome.

Does that mean that the man is wasting his time when he enters the church, or the woman when she steps into the hospital chapel? I think not. I think they gain two things from their prayers, even if they don't get what they are praying for. First, they gain the reassuring knowledge that they are not alone. God is with them in their fear and uncertainty, to help make an uncertain future that much less frightening. The man and the woman are turning to God in prayer in part because they feel they have lost control over their own lives. Things are affecting their lives in which they have little say. They feel alone and helpless. How might God answer their prayers? He might say to the woman in the hospital chapel, "I can't guarantee that your husband will survive this crisis. If I could, no one would ever die because every patient has someone who prays fervently for his recovery. But I can assure you that you are not so alone as you may feel you are. Friends are calling you, people are praying for you, offering to help you. It may well help your husband's chances to know that so many people are rooting for him to pull through. And when you do feel alone and frightened, know that you can always talk to Me, a God who stands for life and healing."

And he might say to the man on his way home from the job search, "I hear your prayer, your fears and hopes. I can't arrange for you to get the job. That's not My role. But I can tell you this. I cherish all of My children, no matter how well or poorly they do in the business world. My way of measuring success has nothing to do with the amount of your salary, the size of your office, or the impressiveness of your job description. And the members of your family, the people who matter the most to you, see you the same way. For Me, that person is successful who has learned how to love, to share, and to master his impulses. I can't give you a job, but I can help you gain a sense of humility if you get the job, and the gift of resiliency and self-respect if you don't, with the reassurance that I am near and think well of you in either event."

Second, prayer is a coming to terms with our limitations. That may be one reason why so many people find it hard to pray today. In this modern age, we are not accustomed to accepting limits. We are more likely to have been raised with the attitude "You can do anything you want if you put your mind to it and work hard enough at it." If that adage is meant to urge us to make the most of our abilities, it is probably true. But at the same time it is also false and misleading. I will never be a professional athlete, a ballet dancer, surgeon, or a poet no matter how much I put my mind to it. It is both cruel and unfair to set me up to blame myself by implying that, if I didn't accomplish something, it was my own fault for not trying hard enough.

When I pray for health, when I pray for world peace, when I pray for the capacity to see other people in a favorable light, one of the things I am doing is acknowledging that there is much that I want and need which I cannot get by my own efforts. I am not so much asking God to give me those things as I am admitting that I cannot attain them without His help. I can probably make myself sick by my own efforts, if I eat, drink, or smoke too much or don't dress warmly in cold weather. But no matter how much I exercise and watch my diet, I can't make myself healthy. I need something beyond my power—call it luck, call it grace—for that. I can make myself obnoxious and unlovable without outside help. I can make other people dislike me. But no matter how rich, smart, or good-looking I may be, and no matter how many books I read on the subject, I can't make someone love me. To ask God for these things is not to order items from a heavenly catalog, but to overcome the illusion of self-sufficiency and confess my dependence.

When do I pray? I try to pray during Sabbath services, but sometimes the responsibility of conducting the service makes that hard. I try to maintain a discipline of personal prayer, but the flesh is weak and the distractions are many. I am most likely to pray in my study, when I have a schedule of counseling appointments. My secretary buzzes me to tell me that my next appointment has arrived—someone with a marital conflict, a problem with a rebellious child, a recent widow who can't get over her depression—and I say to myself, "This person is coming to see me because she has a problem she can't

A MONK PRAYS AT A STATUE OF A RECLINING
BUDDHA IN POLONNARUWA, SRI LANKA.

handle. What makes her think I can help her? I'm not necessarily any wiser than she is." In those moments between receiving the call and opening the door to let the person in, I pray. I pray that I will be worthy of the expectations and the confidence the person is reposing in me. I pray that she will not be disappointed in the value of religion because she does not feel helped by the time she spends with me. I pray that God will grant me the insight and the inspiration to help this person, that He grant me the patience to hear her story without judging her, that He make me a channel for His love and His strength, to share it with those of His children who are in need.

I think we can all learn to pray that way, trusting that when we reach the borders of our own strength and cunning, God will take us by the hand and lead us, unafraid, into new and uncharted territory.

Dr. Gershon Rosenstein, a prominent Russian scientist, a specialist in the chemistry of the brain, discovered religion as an adult and prevailed on the Soviet government to let him go to Israel, where he could practice his newly claimed faith. Shortly after his arrival there. He was interviewed about how a scientist could suddenly accept religion. He said among other things, "I remember the first time I tried to pray, to probe the depths of my heart and reach God. My scientific mind said to me, 'You fool, what are you doing? To whom do you think you are speaking?' To this day, I have a great fear about what would have happened to me if I had not overcome my intellectual hesitations at that moment."

What would have happened to him? He would have spent the rest of his life stuck in the illusion of self-sufficiency, believing that his own strength and intelligence were all he had, and all he would need, to make it through life. In another Hassidic story, the disciple comes to the rabbi and says, "I have a terrible problem. I can't pray. I try to say the words but nothing happens. I don't feel anything. What should I do?" The rabbi answers, "Pray for the ability to pray."

Psalm 73 is a spiritual masterpiece, a favorite of many people who know the Book of Psalms well. It is the account of a man who found himself doubting God because of the world's unfairness and found his answer not in theology but in the experience of God's presence:

God is truly good to Israel,

To whose heart is pure.

As for me, my feet had almost strayed,

My steps were nearly led off course,

For I envied the profligate,

I saw the wicked at ease ...

(I thought to myself) It was for nothing that I kept my heart pure

And washed my hands in innocence,

Seeing that I have been constantly afflicted,

That each morning brings new torments.

Had I decided to say those things,

I should have been false to the circle of Your disciples.

So I applied myself to try to understand this,

But it seemed a hopeless task

Till I entered Your sanctuary ...

You held my right hand,

You guided me by Your counsels

And led me toward honor.

Whom else have I in heaven?

And having You, I want no one on earth.

My mind and my body may fail,

But God is the Rock of my mind, my portion forever.

Those who keep far from You perish ...

But as for me, nearness to God is my good.

[Psalm 73:1-3, 13-17, 23-27]

The author of that deeply moving Psalm begins with an experience many of us have. He sees selfish, wicked people prospering. He sees good things happening to bad people and he wonders, "Was it for nothing that I kept my heart pure?" Are religion and morality just a fraud designed to keep us docile while the wicked take advantage of us? He finds no answer to his question "till I entered [God's] sanctuary." And then, the answer is not an explanation. The answer is the experience of the nearness of God, the experience of feeling that God is taking him by the hand. In the light of that experience, all doubt, all philosophical and intellectual questions melt away. As Martin Buber points out in his commentary on Psalm 73, God answers his questions not by explaining the apparent prosperity of the wicked, but by making him one of the pure of heart. There is still evil in the world and it is still our obligation to oppose it, to expose and punish the wicked. But once we have tasted the presence of God, we will no longer envy the wicked.

What do we get from prayer, if it will not help us choose a winning lottery ticket or achieve a miraculous recovery from illness? We get a sense of being in God's presence, and that can put both our victories and our tragedies in a different perspective.

If we live every moment of our lives in the secular world, we will come to define success and happiness in secular terms. The world will be a battlefield, a constant struggle for advancement and advantage, dividing us into winners and losers. If we pray at all, our prayers will be prayers for victory: "God, give me a place among the winners."

But if we learn the art of entering into God's presence, we will learn to see success and happiness in other, more human terms. Our prayer will not be "Give me this because I deserve it" or "Give me this because I need it." Our prayer will not be the prayer of the jealous child competing for his share of parental love, "Do for me what You have done for others, so I will know that You love me." Our prayer will be the prayer of the author of Psalm 73, asking for nothing but humbly giving thanks. "As for me, nearness to God is my good."

O God, help us in this darkened period of human history to remember once again who we are and what the purpose of our existence is here on earth. We have become usurpers of the human state, parading as human beings without full awareness of what it really means to be human. Rather than being a channel of Thy grace for Thy creation, we have decimated the harmony of life on earth, pushing many of the species (including ours) to the verge of extinction.

O God, awaken us at the beginning of this new era from the dream of negligence and help us to fulfill our responsibilities as representatives of Thy sovereignty here on earth with essential duties toward each other and toward the whole of creation. Help us to remember our true nature, to recall whence we came and wither we shall go. Aid us in the journey of life to do Thy will and to act as the bridge between Heaven and earth, thus fulfilling the role for which Thou didst create us. Shower Thy grace upon us in the moment of our greatest need, protect us from ourselves, and allow us to be a beacon of light rather than a dark cloud for the ambience that surrounds us. Only with Thy aid can we create that peace within and harmony with the outer environment, both natural and social, for which our souls yearn. Only awareness of Thy oneness can prevent us from that idolatry and dispersive multiplicity that destroy all that our inner being seeks. We pray to Thee to help us remain true to our inner selves, to that primordial nature which we still carry in the deep recesses of our souls.

—*Seyyed Hossein Nasr*

The Efficacy of Prayer .... C. S. Lewis

Some years ago I got up one morning intending to have my hair cut in preparation for a visit to London, and the first letter I opened made it clear I need not go to London. So I decided to put the haircut off too. But then there began the most unaccountable little nagging in my mind, almost like a voice saying, "Get it cut all the same. Go and get it cut." In the end I could stand it no longer. I went. Now my barber at that time was a fellow Christian and a man of many troubles whom my brother and I had sometimes been able to help. The moment I opened his shop door he said, "Oh, I was praying you might come today." And in fact if I had come a day or so later I should have been of no use to him.

It awed me; it awes me still. But of course one cannot rigorously prove a causal connection between the barber's prayers and my visit. It might be telepathy. It might be accident.

I have stood by the bedside of a woman whose thighbone was eaten through with cancer and who had thriving colonies of the disease in many other bones as well. It took three people to move her in bed. The doctors predicted a few months of life; the nurses (who often know better), a few weeks. A good man laid his hands on her and prayed. A year later the patient was walking (uphill, too, through rough woodland) and the man who took the last X-ray photos was saying, "These bones are as solid as rock. It's miraculous."

But once again there is no rigorous proof. Medicine, as all true doctors admit, is not an exact science. We need not invoke the supernatural to explain the falsification of its prophecies. You need not, unless you choose, believe in a causal connection between the prayers and the recovery.

The question then arises, "What sort of evidence would prove the efficacy of prayer?" The thing we pray for may happen, but how can you ever know it was not going to happen anyway? Even if the thing were indisputably miraculous it would not follow that the miracle had occurred because of your prayers. The answer surely is that a compulsive empirical proof such as we have in the sciences can never be attained.

Some things are proved by the unbroken uniformity of our experiences. The law of gravitation is established by the fact that, in our experience, all bodies without exception obey it.

A GIRL AND HER GRANDMOTHER PRAY AT THE ALTAR OF SANTO NINO CHURCH IN CEBU, THE PHILIPPINES.

85

HOLY WEEK PROCESSION, ANTIGUA, GUATEMALA.

Now even if all the things that people prayed for happened, which they do not, this would not prove what Christians mean by the efficacy of prayer. For prayer is request. The essence of request, as distinct from compulsion, is that it may or may not be granted. And if an infinitely wise Being listens to the requests of finite and foolish creatures, of course He will sometimes grant and sometimes refuse them. Invariable "success" in prayer would not prove the Christian doctrine at all. It would prove something much more like magic—a power in certain human beings to control, or compel, the course of nature.

There are, no doubt, passages in the New Testament which may seem at first sight to promise an invariable granting of our prayers. But that cannot be what they really mean. For in the very heart of the story we meet a glaring instance to the contrary. In Gethsemane the holiest of all petitioners prayed three times that a certain cup might pass from Him. It did not. After that the idea that prayer is recommended to us as a sort of infallible gimmick may be dismissed.

Other things are proved not simply by experience but by those artificially contrived experiences which we call experiments. Could this be done about prayer? I will pass over the objection that no Christian could take part in such a project, because he has been forbidden it: "You must not try experiments on God, your Master." Forbidden or not, is the thing even possible?

I have seen it suggested that a team of people—the more the better—should agree to pray as hard as they knew how, over a period of six weeks, for all the patients in Hospital A and none of those in Hospital B. Then you would tot up the results and see if A had more cures and fewer deaths. And I suppose you would repeat the experiment at various times and places so as to eliminate the influence of irrelevant factors.

The trouble is that I do not see how any real prayer could go on under such conditions. "Words without thoughts never to heaven go," says the King in *Hamlet.* Simply to say prayers is not to pray; otherwise a team of properly trained parrots would serve as well as men for our experiment. You cannot pray for the recovery of the sick unless the end you have in view is their recovery. But you can have no motive for desiring the recovery of all the patients in one hospital and none of those in another. You are not doing it in order that suffering should be relieved; you are doing it to find out what happens. The real purpose and the nominal purpose of your prayers are at variance. In other words, whatever your tongue and teeth and knees may do, you are not praying. The experiment demands an impossibility.

Empirical proof and disproof are, then, unobtainable. But this conclusion will seem less depressing if we remember that prayer is request and compare it with other specimens of the same thing.

We make requests of our fellow creatures as well as

ABOVE: MASS AT CHRIST THE KING ROMAN CATHOLIC CATHEDRAL IN JOHANNESBURG, SOUTH AFRICA.
OPPOSITE: MORMONS BOW THEIR HEADS IN PRAYER AT A PIONEER RE-ENACTMENT IN UTAH.

of God: we ask for the salt, we ask for a raise in pay, we ask a friend to feed the cat while we are on our holidays, we ask a woman to marry us. Sometimes we get what we ask for and sometimes not. But when we do, it is not nearly so easy as one might suppose to prove with scientific certainty a causal connection between the asking and the getting.

Your neighbor may be a humane person who would not have let your cat starve even if you had forgotten to make any arrangement. Your employer is never so likely to grant your request for a raise as when he is aware that you could get better money from a rival firm and is quite possibly intending to secure you by a raise in any case. As for the lady who consents to marry you—are you sure she had not decided to do so already? Your proposal, you know, might have been the result, not the cause, of her decision. A certain important conversation might never have taken place unless she had intended that it should.

Thus in some measure the same doubt that hangs about the causal efficacy of our prayers to God hangs also about our prayers to man. Whatever we get we might have been going to get anyway. But only, as I say, in some measure. Our friend, boss, and wife may tell us that they acted because we asked; and we may know them so well as to feel sure, first that they are saying what they believe to be true, and secondly that they understand their own motives well enough to be right. But notice that when this happens our assurance has not been gained by the methods of science. We do not try the control experiment of refusing the raise or breaking off the engagement and then making our request again under fresh conditions. Our assurance is different in kind from scientific knowledge. It is born out of our personal relation to the other parties; not from knowing things about them but from knowing them.

Our assurance—if we reach an assurance—that God always hears and sometimes grants our prayers, and that apparent grantings are not merely fortuitous, can only come in the same sort of way. There can be no question of tabulating successes and failures and trying to decide whether the successes are too numerous to be accounted for by chance. Those who best know a man

best know whether, when he did what they asked, he did it because they asked. I think those who best know God will best know whether He sent me to the barber's shop because the barber prayed.

For up till now we have been tackling the whole question in the wrong way and on the wrong level. The very question "Does prayer work?" puts us in the wrong frame of mind from the outset. "Work": as if it were magic, or a machine—something that functions automatically. Prayer is either a sheer illusion or a personal contact between embryonic, incomplete persons (ourselves) and the utterly concrete Person. Prayer in the sense of petition, asking for things, is a small part of it; confession and penitence are its threshold, adoration its sanctuary, the presence and vision and enjoyment of God its bread and wine. In it God shows Himself to us. That He answers prayers is a corollary—not necessarily the most important one—from that revelation. What He does is learned from what He is.

Petitionary prayer is, nonetheless, both allowed and commanded to us: "Give us our daily bread." And no doubt it raises a theoretical problem. Can we believe that God ever really modifies His action in response to the suggestions of men? For infinite wisdom does not need telling what is best, and infinite goodness needs no urging to do it. But neither does God need any of those things that are done by finite agents, whether living or inanimate. He could, if He chose, repair our bodies miraculously without food; or give us food without the aid of farmers, bakers, and butchers; or knowledge without the aid of learned men; or convert the heathen without missionaries. Instead, He allows soils and weather and animals and the muscles, minds, and wills of men to co-operate in the execution of His will. "God," said Pascal, "instituted prayer in order to lend to His creatures the dignity of causality." But not only prayer; whenever we act at all He lends us that dignity. It is not really stranger, nor less strange, that my prayers should affect the course of events than that my other actions should do so. They have not advised or changed God's mind—that is, His over-all purpose. But that purpose will be realized in different ways according to the actions, including the prayers, of His creatures.

For He seems to do nothing of Himself which He can possibly delegate to His creatures. He commands us to do slowly and blunderingly what He could do perfectly and in the twinkling of an eye. He allows us to neglect what He would have us do, or to fail. Perhaps we do not fully realize the problem, so to call it, of enabling finite free wills to co-exist with Omnipotence. It seems to involve at every moment almost a sort of divine abdication. We are not mere recipients or spectators. We are either privileged to share in the game or compelled to collaborate in the work, "to wield our little tridents." Is this amazing process simply Creation going on before our eyes? This is how (no light matter) God makes something—indeed, makes Gods—out of nothing.

So at least it seems to me. But what I have offered can be, at the very best, only a mental model or symbol. All that we say on such subjects must be merely analogical and parabolic. The reality is doubtless not comprehensible by our faculties. But we can at any rate try to expel bad analogies and bad parables. Prayer is not a machine. It is not magic. It is not advice offered to God. Our act, when we pray, must not, any more than all our other acts, be separated from the continuous act of God Himself, in which alone all finite causes operate.

It would be even worse to think of those who get what they pray for as a sort of court favorites, people who have influence with the throne. The refused prayer of Christ in Gethsemane is answer enough to that. And I dare not leave out the hard saying which I once heard from an experienced Christian: "I have seen many striking answers to prayer and more than one that I thought miraculous. But they usually come at the beginning: before conversion, or soon after it. As the Christian life proceeds, they tend to be rarer. The refusals, too, are not only more frequent; they become more unmistakable, more emphatic."

Does God then forsake just those who serve Him best? Well, He who served Him best of all said, near His tortured death, "Why hast thou forsaken me?" When God becomes man, that Man, of all others, is least comforted by God, at His greatest need. There is a mystery here which, even if I had the power, I might not have the courage to explore. Meanwhile, little people like you and me, if our prayers are sometimes granted, beyond all hope and probability, had better not draw hasty conclusions to our own advantage. If we were stronger, we might be less tenderly treated. If we were braver we might be sent, with far less help, to defend far more desperate posts in the great battle.

"*True prayer never goes unanswered. It does not mean that every little thing we ask for from God is readily given to us. It is only when we shed our selfishness…and approach God in true humility that our prayers find a response.*"

Mohandas K. Gandhi

An offering of incense at Meenakshi Temple in Madurai, India.

Foolish Prayer .... Carol Zaleski

Six years before he died, American philosopher William James filled out a questionnaire about religious experience. He was asked, among other things, "Do you pray?" His answer was forthright: "I can't possibly pray. I feel foolish and artificial." And yet James wrote, in *The Varieties of Religious Experience,* that prayer is "the very soul and essence of religion" and that in prayer "work is really done, and spiritual energy flows in and produces effects." It's well known that James longed to experience such effects in his own life, yet he remained trapped in his pragmatic corridor, generously holding open the door to prayer for others but unable to enter it himself.

I wonder if it ever occurred to William James that feeling foolish and artificial is as good a starting point as any for prayer. Prayer is like courtship; of course it feels foolish and artificial. It's not something you can work out inwardly and then execute outwardly. It's a series of improbable and ungainly gestures, learned by imitation, that make it possible to fall in love. Perhaps I see it this way because as a chronic beginner at prayer, I often feel foolish and inept.

Lately I have been learning about prayer-courtship from the rosary. What could be more improbable and ungainly than this prayer of incessant repetition, learned by imitation and practiced by rote?

According to Friedrich Heiler's 1932 classic *Prayer,* rote prayer is a sign of hardening of the spiritual arteries: "Prayer is at first a spontaneous emotional discharge, a free outpouring of the heart. In the course of development it becomes a fixed formula which people recite without feeling or mood of devotion, untouched both in heart and mind. At first prayer is an intimate intercourse with God, but gradually it becomes hard, impersonal, ceremonial, a rite consecrated by ancestral custom ...Even among primitive peoples this process of petrification and mechanization ...transforms free prayer into precise and rigid formulas."

To many Christians the rosary embodies all the vices of "petrification" to which Heiler alludes: precise and rigid formulas, vain repetition, conformity, credulity and works-righteousness, compounded by Mariolatry, triumphalism and superstition. Many have been ready to see the

A ROMAN CATHOLIC
WOMAN PRAYS THE
ROSARY.

practice die out—not only Protestants who consider the petrification of prayer a peculiarly Petrine liability, but also Catholics for whom the rosary is like a woolly mammoth blocking the door to liturgical reform.

But it hasn't died out. How many thousand Hail Marys, Our Fathers and Glory Bes are being struck on the rosary strings at this instant across the globe? The rosary encircles the world like a magnificent Tibetan prayer wheel, spinning out adoration. It's a giant carousel you can climb upon at any point and step off again, knowing that the prayer will keep going with or without you; tradition has seen it as the liturgy in miniature, mirroring in its 15 decades the 150 psalms, as a potent means of intercession, a weapon against the forces of darkness, a reparation for human sin, and a tried-and-true means of initiation into the mysteries of Christ. Like the Jesus Prayer of the Christian East, the rosary is cherished as a compendium of the Gospels, a temple of the divine name and a heaven-sent method for fulfilling the biblical injunction to "pray without ceasing."

The rosary is also a school of prayer for lifelong beginners like me, and increasingly it is being rediscovered as a way of prayer for all Christians. Within the Anglican communion it has flourished for some time. Evelyn Underhill loved the rosary and so did Austin Farrer. John Macquarrie commends it in his book *Mary for All Christians*. With his apostolic letter of [October 2002], *Rosarium Virginis Mariae,* Pope John Paul II set a small fire under this process of ecumenical rediscovery by offering an intensely Christocentric and contemplative interpretation of the rosary. Most remarkably, he introduced a fourth series of mysteries on which to meditate: the *lucis mysteriis,* or "mysteries of light," focusing on events in the public ministry of Jesus Christ: his baptism in the Jordan, first miracle at Cana, preaching of the kingdom, transfiguration, and institution of the Eucharist.

According to the pope, the rosary is a Christian *zakar* (remembrance) of Christ through Mary. One thinks of the Sufi *zikr,* remembrance of God through repetitive prayer. My Tibetan friend Dechen practices *buddhanusmrti,* remembrance of the Buddha, with the aid of his 108-bead rosary. To outsiders such practices may look like mumbo-jumbo, but those who pray them know how they can train the spirit to make a free and loving response to the divine call. Our heart beats repetitively while our mind wanders. The rosary brings the straying mind down to the repeating heart, quiets the mind and centers the gaze, with Mary, on the face of her beloved son.

"Pray as you can," John Chapman used to say, "not as you can't." We can be dry as dust, bored, distracted and insensible to God's presence. Still we can pray, mechanically if need be, taking refuge in whatever means have been given. We can rest on the rosary as a climber rests on his fixed rope—it's safe to dangle as long as the rope is anchored in rock. We may not have a mystical bone in our bodies, but no matter. God is waiting for us, and if we make even the smallest gesture of availability he will be there, whether we feel his presence or not.

ABOVE: A CATHOLIC NUN IN RAPTUROUS
PRAYER DURING A MASS CELEBRATED BY
POPE JOHN PAUL II AT CIUDAD TRUJILLO IN
THE DOMINICAN REPUBLIC.
FOLLOWING PAGES: TIBETAN PILGRIMS PAUSE
FOR A SUNSET PRAYER.

Lord, the day is already waning, stay with us.

Stay to illuminate our doubts and our fears.

Stay so that we may fortify our light with yours.

Stay to help us be strong and generous.

Stay so that in a world that has little faith and hope we may be

able to encourage one another and sow faith and hope.

Stay so that we, too, may learn from you to be the light for other

young people and for the world.

—Pope John Paul II

The Still, Silent Moment

QUIETING THE MIND DRAWS US NEARER TO THE SACRED WITHIN OURSELVES

What Is Meditation? .... Thomas Merton

To meditate is to exercise the mind in serious reflection. This is the broadest possible sense of the word "meditation." The term in this sense is not confined to religious reflections, but it implies serious mental activity and a certain absorption or concentration which does not permit our faculties to wander off at random or to remain slack and undirected.

From the very start it must be made clear, however, that reflection here does not refer to a purely intellectual activity, and still less does it refer to mere reasoning. Reflection involves not only the mind but also the heart, and indeed our whole being. One who really meditates does not merely think, he also loves, and by his love—or at least by his sympathetic intuition into the reality upon which he reflects—he enters into that reality and knows it so to speak from within, by a kind of identification.

St. Thomas and St. Bernard of Clairvaux describe meditation (*consideratio*) as "the quest for truth." Nevertheless their "meditation" is something quite distinct from study, which is also a "quest for truth." Meditation and study can, of course, be closely related. In fact, study is not spiritually fruitful unless it leads to some kind of meditation. By study we seek the truth in books or in some other source outside our own minds. In meditation we strive to absorb what we have already taken in. We consider the principles we have learned and we apply them to our own lives. Instead of simply storing up facts and ideas in our memory, we strive to do some original thinking of our own.

In study we can be content with an idea or a concept that is true. We can be content to know *about* truth. Meditation is for those who are not satisfied with a merely objective and conceptual knowledge *about* life, *about* God—*about* ultimate realities. They want to enter into an intimate contact with truth itself, with God. They want to experience the deepest realities of life by *living* them. Meditation is the means to that end.

And so, although the definition of meditation as a quest for truth (*inquisitio veritatis*) brings out the fact that meditation is above all a function of the intelligence, nevertheless it implies something more. St. Thomas and St. Bernard were speaking of a kind of meditation which is fundamentally religious, or at least philosophical, and which aims at bringing our

A BUDDHIST MONK
IN MEDITATION.

"Absolutely unmixed attention is prayer."
Simone Weil

RUSSIAN ORTHODOX NUNS PRAY OVER AN
ICON DURING AN EASTER CELEBRATION IN
JERUSALEM.

whole being into communication with an ultimate reality beyond and above ourselves. This unitive and loving knowledge begins in meditation but it reaches its full development only in contemplative prayer.

This idea is very important. Strictly speaking, even religious meditation is primarily a matter of thought. But it does not end in thought. Meditative thought is simply the beginning of a process which leads to interior prayer and is normally supposed to culminate in contemplation and in affective communion with God. We can call this whole process (in which meditation leads to contemplation) by the name *mental prayer*. In actual practice, the word "meditation" is quite often used as if it meant exactly the same thing as "mental prayer." But if we look at the precise meaning of the word, we find that meditation is only a small part of the whole complex of interior activities which go to make up mental prayer. Meditation is the name given to the earlier part of the process, the part in which our heart and mind exercise themselves in a series of interior activities which prepare us for union with God.

When thought is without affective intention, when it begins and ends in the intelligence, it does not lead to prayer, to love or to communion. Therefore it does not fall into the proper pattern of mental prayer. Such thought is not really meditation. It is outside the sphere of religion and of prayer. It is therefore excluded from our consideration here. It has nothing to do with our subject. We need only remark that a person would be wasting his time if he thought reasoning alone could satisfy the need of his soul for spiritual meditation. Meditation is not merely a matter of "thinking things out," even if that leads to a good ethical resolution. Meditation is more than mere practical thinking.

The distinctive characteristic of religious meditation is that it is a search for truth which springs from love and which seeks to possess the truth not only by knowledge but also by love. It is, therefore, an intellectual activity which is inseparable from an intense consecration of spirit and application of the will. The presence of *love* in our meditation intensifies and clarifies our thought by giving it a deeply affective quality. Our meditation becomes charged with a loving appreciation of the *value* hidden in the supreme truth which the intelligence is seeking. This affective drive of the will, seeking the truth as the soul's highest good, raises the soul above the level of speculation and makes our quest for truth a prayer full of reverential love and adoration striving to pierce the dark cloud which stands between us and the throne of God. We beat against this cloud with supplication, we lament our poverty, our helplessness, we adore the mercy of God and His supreme perfections, we dedicate ourselves entirely to His worship.

Mental prayer is therefore something like a skyrocket. Kindled by a spark of divine love, the soul streaks heavenward in an act of intelligence as clear and direct as the rocket's trail of fire. Grace has released all the deepest energies of our spirit and assists us to climb to new and unsuspected heights. Nevertheless, our own faculties soon reach their limit. The intelligence can climb no higher into the sky. There is a point where the mind bows down its fiery trajectory as if to acknowledge its limitations and proclaim the infinite supremacy of the unattainable God.

But it is here that our "meditation" reaches its climax. Love again takes the initiative and the rocket "explodes" in a burst of sacrificial praise. Thus love flings out a hundred burning stars, acts of all kinds, expressing everything that is best in man's spirit, and the soul spends itself in drifting fires that glorify the Name of God while they fall earthward and die away in the night wind!

That is why St. Albert the Great, the master who gave St. Thomas Aquinas his theological formation at Paris and Cologne, contrasts the contemplation of the philosopher and the contemplation of the saints: "The contemplation of philosophers seeks nothing but the

perfection of the one contemplating and it goes no further than the intellect. But the contemplation of the saints is fired by the love of the one contemplated: That is, God. Therefore it does not terminate in an act of the intelligence but passes over into the will by love. St. Thomas Aquinas, his disciple, remarks tersely that for this very reason the contemplative's knowledge of God is arrived at, on this earth, by the light of burning love: *per ardorem caritatis datur cognitio veritatis.*" (Commentary on St. John's Gospel, Chapter 5.)

The contemplation of "philosophers," which is merely intellectual speculation on the divine nature as it is reflected in creatures, would be therefore like a skyrocket that soared into the sky but never went off. The beauty of the rocket is in its "death," and the beauty of mental prayer and of mystical contemplation is in the soul's abandonment and total surrender of itself in an outburst of praise in which it spends itself entirely to bear witness to the transcendent goodness of the infinite God. The rest is silence.

Let us never forget that the fruitful silence in which words lose their power and concepts escape our grasp is perhaps the perfection of meditation. We need not fear and become restless when we are no longer able to "make acts." Rather we should rejoice and rest in the luminous darkness of faith. This "resting" is a higher way of prayer.

Training the Puppy: Mindfulness of Breathing .... Jack Kornfield

A story is told of the Buddha when he was wandering in India shortly after his enlightenment. He was encountered by several men who recognized something quite extraordinary about this handsome prince now robed as a monk. Stopping to inquire, they asked, "Are you a god?" "No," he answered. "Well, are you a deva or an angel?" "No," he replied. "Well, are you some kind of wizard or magician?" "No." "Are you a man?" "No." They were perplexed. Finally they asked, "Then what are you?" He replied simply, "I am awake." The word Buddha means to awaken. How to awaken is all he taught.

Meditation can be thought of as the art of awakening. Through the mastering of this art we can learn new ways to approach our difficulties and bring wisdom and joy alive in our life. Through developing meditation's tools and practices, we can awaken the best of our spiritual, human capacities. The key to this art is the steadiness of our attention. When the fullness of our attention is cultivated together with a grateful and tender heart, our spiritual life will naturally grow.

As we have seen, some healing of mind and body must take place for many of us before we can sit quietly and concentrate. Yet even to begin our healing, to begin understanding ourselves, we must have some basic level of attention. To deepen our practice further, we must choose a way to develop our attention systematically and give ourselves to it quite fully. Otherwise we will drift like a boat without a rudder. To learn to concentrate we must choose a prayer or meditation and follow this path with commitment and steadiness, a willingness to work with our practice day after day, no matter what arises. This is not easy for most people. They would like their spiritual life to show immediate and cosmic results. But what great art is ever learned quickly? Any deep training opens in direct proportion to how much we give ourselves to it.

Consider the other arts. Music, for example. How long would it take to learn to play the piano well? Suppose we take months or years of lessons once a week, practicing diligently every day. Initially, almost everyone struggles to learn which fingers go for which notes and how to read basic lines of music. However, to master the art so that we could play music well,

alone or in a group, or join a band or an orchestra, we would have to give ourselves to this discipline over and over, time and again. If we wanted to learn computer programming, oil painting, tennis, architecture, any of the thousand arts, we would have to give ourselves to it fully and wholeheartedly over a long period of time—a training, an apprenticeship, a cultivation.

Nothing less is required in the spiritual arts. Perhaps even more is asked. Yet through this mastery we master ourselves and our lives. We learn the most human art, how to connect with our truest self.

Trungpa Rinpoche called spiritual practice manual labor. It is a labor of love in which we bring a whole-hearted attention to our own situation over and over again. In all sorts of weather, we steady and deepen our prayer, meditation, and discipline, learning how to see with honesty and compassion, how to let go, how to love more deeply.

However, this is not how we begin. Suppose we begin with a period of solitude in the midst of our daily life. What happens when we actually try to meditate? The most frequent first experience—whether in prayer or chanting, meditation or visualization—is that we encounter the disconnected and scattered mind. Buddhist psychology likens the untrained mind to a crazed monkey that dashes from thought to memory, from sight to sound, from plan to regret without ceasing. If we were able to sit quietly for an hour and fully observe all the places our mind went, what a script would be revealed.

When we first undertake the art of meditation, it is indeed frustrating. Inevitably, as our mind wanders and our body feels the tension it has accumulated and the speed to which it is addicted, we often see how little inner discipline, patience, or compassion we actually have. It doesn't take much time with a spiritual task to see how scattered and unsteady our attention remains even when we try to direct and focus it. While we usually think of it as "our mind," if we look honestly, we see that the mind follows its own nature, conditions, and laws. Seeing this, we also see that we must gradually discover a wise relationship to the mind that connects it to the body and heart, and steadies and calms our inner life.

The essence of this connecting is the bringing back of our attention again and again to the practice we have chosen. Prayer, meditation, repeating sacred phrases, or visualization gives us a systematic way to focus and steady our concentration. All the traditional realms and states of consciousness described in mystical and spiritual literature worldwide are arrived at through the art of concentration. These arts of concentration,

ABOVE: HINDUS AND BUDDHISTS OFTEN USE FINGER GESTURES, OR MUDRAS, IN THEIR MEDITATION PRACTICE TO ENHANCE CONCENTRATION AND INVOKE THE DIVINE.

of returning to the task at hand, also bring the clarity, strength of mind, peacefulness, and profound connectedness that we seek. This steadiness and connection in turn gives rise to even deeper levels of understanding and insight.

Whether a practice calls for visualization, question, prayer, sacred words, or simple meditation on feelings or breath, it always involves the steadying and conscious return, again and again, to some focus. As we learn to do this with a deeper and fuller attention, it is like learning to steady a canoe in waters that have waves. Repeating our meditation, we relax and sink into the moment, deeply connecting with what is present. We let ourselves settle into a spiritual ground; we train ourselves to come back to this moment. This is a patient process. St. Francis de Sales said, "What we need is a cup of understanding, a barrel of love, and an ocean of patience."

For some, this task of coming back a thousand or ten thousand times in meditation may seem boring or even of questionable importance. But how many times have we gone away from the reality of our life? —perhaps a million or ten million times! If we wish to awaken, we have to find our way back here with our full being, our full attention.

St. Francis de Sales continued by saying: "Bring yourself back to the point quite gently. And even if you do nothing during the whole of your hour but bring your heart back a thousand times, though it went away every time you brought it back, your hour would be very well employed."

In this way, meditation is very much like training a puppy. You put the puppy down and say, "Stay." Does the puppy listen? It gets up and it runs away. You sit the puppy back down again. "Stay." And the puppy runs away over and over again. Sometimes the puppy jumps up, runs over, and pees in the corner or makes some other mess. Our minds are much the same as the puppy, only they create even bigger messes. In training the mind, or the puppy, we have to start over and over again.

When you undertake a spiritual discipline, frustration comes with the territory. Nothing in our culture or our schooling has taught us to steady and calm our attention. One psychologist has called us a society of attentional spastics. Finding it difficult to concentrate, many people respond by forcing their attention on their breath or mantra or prayer with tense irritation and self-judgment, or worse. Is this the way you would train a puppy? Does it really help to beat it? Concentration is never a matter of force or coercion. You simply pick up the puppy again and return to reconnect with the here and now.

Developing a deep quality of interest in your spiritual practice is one of the keys to the whole art of concentration. Steadiness is nourished by the degree of interest with which we focus our meditation. Yet, to the beginning student, many meditation subjects appear plain and uninteresting. There is a traditional story about a Zen student who complained to his master that following the breath was boring. The Zen master grabbed this student and held his head under water for quite a long time while the student struggled to come up. When he finally let the student up, the Zen master asked him whether he had found breath boring in those moments under water.

Concentration combines full interest with delicacy of attention. This attention should not be confused with being removed or detached. Awareness does not mean separating ourselves from experience; it means allowing it and sensing it fully. Awareness can vary like a zoom lens. Sometimes we are in the middle of our experience. Sometimes it is as if we sit on our own shoulder and notice what is present, and sometimes we can be aware with a great spacious distance. All of these are useful aspects of awareness. They each can help us sense and touch and see our life more clearly from moment to moment. As we learn to steady the quality of our attention, it is accompanied by a deeper and deeper sense of stillness—poised, exquisite, and subtle.

The art of subtle attention was learned by one meditation student while she and her husband lived in a remote community in the mountains of British Columbia. She had studied yoga in India, and some years later she, with the help of her husband, gave birth to a baby boy, alone, without doctor or midwife. Unfortunately, it was a long and complicated breech delivery, with the baby delivered feetfirst and the umbilical cord wrapped around his neck. The baby was born quite blue, and he could not start to breathe on his own. His parents gave him infant artificial respiration as best they could. Then they would pause for a moment between their breathing into his lungs to see if he would begin to breathe by himself. During these excruciating moments, they watched for the tiniest movement of his breath to see if he would live or die. Finally, he started to breathe on his own. His mother smiled at me when she told this story, and said, "It was at that time that I learned what it meant to be truly aware of the breath. And it wasn't even my own breath!"

The focusing of attention on the breath is perhaps the most universal of the many hundreds of meditation subjects used worldwide. Steadying attention on the movement of the life-breath is central to yoga, to Buddhist and Hindu practices, to Sufi, Christian, and Jewish traditions. While other meditation subjects are

SHWEDAGON PAGODA IN YANGON, MYANMAR.

"The world is holy. We are holy. All life is holy.
Daily prayers are delivered on the lips of breaking waves,
the whisperings of grasses, the shimmering of leaves."

Terry Tempest Williams

A HINDU WOMAN PRAYS TO THE RISING SUN
NEAR THE HOLY CITY OF PURI, INDIA.

also beneficial, and each has its unique qualities, we will continue to elaborate on the practice of breath meditation as an illustration for developing any of these practices. Breathing meditation can quiet the mind, open the body, and develop a great power of concentration. The breath is available to us at any time of day and in any circumstance. When we have learned to use it, the breath becomes a support for awareness throughout our life.

But awareness of breathing does not come right away. At first we must sit quietly, letting our body be relaxed and alert, and simply practice finding the breath in the body. Where do we actually feel it—as a coolness in the nose, a tingling in the back of the throat, as a movement in the chest, as a rise and fall of the belly? The place of strongest feeling is the first place to establish our attention. If the breath is apparent in several places, we can feel its whole movement of the body. If the breath is too soft and difficult to find, we can place our palm on our belly and feel the expansion and contraction in our hand. We must learn to focus our attention carefully. As we feel each breath we can sense how it moves in our body. Do not try to control the breath, only notice its natural movement, as a gatekeeper notices what passes by. What are its rhythms? Is it shallow or long and deep? Does it become fast or slow? Is there a temperature to the breath? The breath can become a great teacher because it is always moving and changing. In this simple breathing, we can learn about contraction and resistance, about opening and letting go. Here we can feel what it means to live gracefully, to sense the truth of the river of energy and change that we are.

Yet even with interest and a strong desire to steady our attention, distractions will arise. Distractions are the natural movement of mind. Distractions arise because our mind and heart are not initially clear or pure. Mind is more like muddy or turbulent water. Each time an enticing image or an interesting memory floats by, it is our habit to react, to get entangled, or to get lost. When painful images or feelings arise, it is our habit to avoid them and unknowingly distract ourselves. We can feel the power of these habits of desire, of distracting ourselves, of fear and reaction. In many of us these forces are so great that after a few unfamiliar moments of calm, our mind rebels. Again and again restlessness, busyness, plans, unfelt feelings, all interrupt our focus. Working with these distractions, steadying the canoe, letting the waves pass by, and coming back again and again in a quiet and collected way, is at the heart of meditation.

After your initial trial, you will begin to recognize that certain external conditions are particularly helpful in developing concentration. Finding or creating a quiet and undistracting place for your practice is necessary. Select regular and suitable times that best fit your temperament and schedule; experiment to discover whether morning or evening meditations best support the silent aspects of your inner life. You may wish to begin with a short period of inspiring reading before sitting, or do some stretching or yoga first. Some people find it extremely helpful to sit in a regular group with others or to go off to periodic retreats. Experiment with these external factors until you discover which are most helpful for your own inner peace. Then make them a regular part of your life. Creating suitable conditions means living wisely, providing the best soil for our spiritual hearts to be nourished and to grow.

As we give ourselves to the art of concentration over

A MONK OF THE KEGON SECT OF BUDDHISM
MEDITATES NEAR HWAOM-SA TEMPLE IN
SOUTH KOREA.

the weeks and months, we discover that our concentration slowly begins to settle by itself. Initially we may have struggled to focus, trying to hold on to the subject of our meditation. Then gradually the mind and the heart become eased from distractions, and periodically we sense them as purer, more workable and malleable. We feel our breath more often and more clearly, or we recite our prayers or mantra with greater wholeness. This is like beginning to read a book. When we start, we will often be interrupted by many distractions around us. But if it is a good book, perhaps a mystery novel, by the last chapter we will be so absorbed in the plot that people can walk right by us and we will not notice them. In meditation at first, thoughts carry us away and we think them for a long time. Then, as concentration grows we remember our breath in the middle of a thought. Later we can notice thoughts just as they arise or allow them to pass in the background, so focused on the breath that we are undisturbed by their movement.

As we continue, the development of concentration brings us closer to life, like the focusing of a lens. When we look at pond water in a cup, it appears clear and still. But under the simplest microscope it shows itself to be alive with creatures and movement. In the same way, the more deeply we pay attention, the less solid our breath and body become. Every place we feel breath in our body can come alive with subtle vibrations, movement, tingles, flow. The steady power of our concentration shows each part of our life to be in change and flux, like a river, even as we feel it.

As we learn to let go into the present, the breath breathes itself, allowing the flow of sensations in the body to move and open. There can come an openness and ease. Like a skilled dancer, we allow the breath and

"In prayer, come empty, do nothing."

St. John of the Cross

BOUDHANATH STUPA, A CENTER OF TIBETAN
BUDDHISM, IN KATHMANDU, NEPAL.

body to float and move unhindered, yet all the while being present to enjoy the opening.

As we become more skillful we also discover that concentration has its own seasons. Sometimes we sit and settle easily. At other times the conditions of mind and body are turbulent or tense. We can learn to navigate all these waters. When conditions show the mind is tight, we learn to soften and relax, to open the attention. When the mind is sleepy or flabby, we learn to sit up and focus with more energy. The Buddha compared this with the tuning of a lute, sensing when we are out of tune and gently strengthening or loosening our energy to come into balance.

In learning concentration, we feel as if we are always starting over, always losing our focus. But where have we actually gone? It is only that a mood or a thought or doubt has swept through our mind. As soon as we recognize this, we can let go and settle back again in this next moment. We can always begin again. Gradually as our interest grows and our capacity to sense deepens, new layers of our meditation open. We will find ourselves alternating, discovering periods of deep peace like an undisturbed child and strength like a great ship on a true course, only to be distracted or lost sometime later. Concentration grows in a deepening spiral, as we return to our meditation subject again and again, each time learning more of the art of inner listening. When we are listening carefully, we can sense new aspects of our breath all the time. One Burmese meditation teacher requires his students each day to tell him something new about the breath, even if they have been meditating for years.

Here, notice if you can, is there a pause between your breaths? How does it feel when your breath just starts? What is the end of the breath like? What is that space when the breathing has stopped? What does the impulse to breathe feel like before the breath even begins? How is the breath a reflection of your moods?

At first when we feel the breath, it seems like only one small movement, but as we develop the art of concentration, we can feel a hundred things in the breath: the subtlest sensations, the variations in its length, the temperature, the swirl, the expansion, the contraction, the tingles that come along with it, the echoes of the breath in different parts of our body, and so much more.

Sticking with a spiritual training requires an ocean of patience because our habit of wanting to be somewhere else is so strong. We've distracted ourselves from the present for so many moments, for so many years, even lifetimes. Here is an accomplishment in *The Guinness Book of World Records* that I like to note at meditation retreats when people are feeling frustrated. It indicates that the record for persistence in taking and failing a driving test is held by Mrs. Miriam Hargrave of Wakefield, England. Mrs. Hargrave failed her thirty-ninth driving test in April, 1970, when she crashed, driving through a set of red lights. In August of the following year she finally passed her fortieth test. Unfortunately, she could no longer afford to buy a car because she had spent so much on driving lessons. In the same spirit, Mrs. Fanny Turner of Little Rock, Arkansas, passed her written test for a driver's license on her 104th attempt in October 1978. If we can bring such persistence to passing a driving test or mastering the art of skateboarding or any one of a hundred other endeavors, surely we can also master the art of connecting with ourselves. As human beings we can dedicate ourselves to almost anything, and this heartfelt perseverance and dedication brings spiritual practice alive.

Always remember that in training a puppy we want to end up with the puppy as our friend. In the same way, we must practice seeing our mind and body as "friend." Even its wanderings can be included in our meditation with a friendly interest and curiosity. Right away we can notice how it moves. The mind produces waves. Our breath is a wave, the sensations of our body are a wave. We don't have to fight the waves. We can simply acknowledge, "Surf's up." "Here's the wave of memories from three years old." "Here's the planning wave." Then it's time to reconnect with the wave of the breath. It takes a gentleness and a kindhearted understanding to deepen the art of concentration. We can't be present for a long period without actually softening, dropping into our bodies, coming to rest. Any other kind of concentration, achieved by force and tension, will only be short-lived. Our task is to train the puppy to become our lifelong friend.

The attitude or spirit with which we do our meditation helps us perhaps more than any other aspect. What is called for is a sense of perseverance and dedication combined with a basic friendliness. We need a willingness to directly relate again and again to what is actually here, with a lightness of heart and sense of humor. We do not want the training of our puppy to become too serious a matter.

The Christian Desert Fathers tell of a new student who was commanded by his master that for three years he must give money to everyone who insulted him. When this period of trial was over, the master said, "Now you can go to Alexandria and truly learn wisdom." When the student entered Alexandria, he met a certain wise man whose way of teaching was to sit at the city gate insulting everyone who came and went. He naturally insulted the student also, who immediately burst out laughing. "Why do you laugh when I insult you?" said the wise man. "Because," said the student, "for years I've been paying for this kind of thing, and now you give it to me for free!" "Enter the city," said the wise man. "It is all yours."

Meditation is a practice that can teach us to enter each moment with wisdom, lightness, and a sense of humor. It is an art of opening and letting go, rather than accumulation or struggle. Then, even within our frustrations and difficulties, a remarkable inner sense of support and perspective can grow. Breathing in, "Wow, this experience is interesting, isn't it? Let me take another breath. Ah, this one is difficult, even terrifying, isn't it?" Breathing out, "Ah." It is an amazing process we have entered when we can train our hearts and minds to be open and steady and awake through it all.

BUDDHIST MONKS STAND IN MEDITATION AT
THE CHURCH OF THE NATIVITY IN BETHLEHEM
ON THE WEST BANK, WHICH COMMEMORATES
THE BIRTHPLACE OF JESUS CHRIST.

May all beings have happiness, and the causes of happiness;

May all be free from sorrow, and the causes of sorrow;

May all never be separated from the sacred happiness which is sorrowless;

And may all live in equanimity, without too much attachment and too much aversion,

And live believing in the equality of all that lives.

—Buddhist prayer

Stillness .... Desmond Tutu

Dear Child of God, all of us are meant to be contemplatives. Frequently we assume that this is reserved for some rare monastic life, lived by special people who alone have been called by God. But the truth of the matter is that each one of us is meant to have that space inside where we can hear God's voice. God is available to all of us. God says, "Be still and know that I am God." Each one of us wants and needs to give ourselves space for quiet. We can hear God's voice most clearly when we are quiet, uncluttered, undistracted—when we are still. Be still, be quiet, and then you begin to see with the eyes of the heart.

One image that I have of the spiritual life is of sitting in front of a fire on a cold day. We don't have to do anything. We just have to sit in front of the fire and then gradually the qualities of the fire are transferred to us. We begin to feel the warmth. We become the attributes of the fire. It's like that with us and God. As we take time to be still and to be in God's presence, the qualities of God are transferred to us.

Far too frequently we see ourselves as doers. As we've seen, we feel we must endlessly work and achieve. We have not always learned just to be receptive, to be in the presence of God, quiet, available, and letting God be God, who wants us to be God. We're shocked, actually, when we hear that what God wants is for us to be godlike, for us to become more and more like God. Not by doing anything, but by letting God be God in and through us.

I am deeply thankful for those moments in the early morning when I try to be quiet, to sit in the presence of the gentle and compassionate and unruffled One to try to share in or be given some of that divine serenity. If I do not spend a reasonable amount of time in meditation early in the morning, then I feel a physical discomfort—it is worse than having forgotten to brush my teeth! I would be completely rudderless and lost if I did not have these times with God.

People often ask about the source of my joy and I can honestly say that it comes from my spiritual life—and specifically from these times of stillness. They are an indispensable part of my day regardless of what else I might face. I pray out loud or to myself before every meeting, and before every drive in the car. I also take quiet days when I do not talk—at least until supper. Once a month I take a room at a local convent and spend a day sleeping, eating, praying, and reading, and at least once a year I go on a retreat of three or more days. The importance of these retreats is hard to convey—through them I am strengthened and am able to hear what God is saying and to seek solutions to problems that seem unsolvable. You may think that as a priest I need these times of reflection but that most people who spend their lives in the marketplace do not. In truth, they probably need them all the more, since the noise of the market makes it even more difficult to hear the voice of God.

I know no other way available to us besides prayer and meditation to cultivate a real and deeply personal relationship with God, our great Lover in whose presence we want to luxuriate, falling into ever greater and deeper silence. This is the silence of love, the stillness of adoration and contemplation—the sort of stillness that is so eloquent when it happens between two who are in love.

When people begin to pray and to meditate, they inevitably focus on technique. They wonder what they should do, and there are many techniques they can choose from. One that I have used over the years is visualizing actually being present at the events retold in the Gospels. But prayer and meditation are not about doing but about being, and the important thing is not to let techniques dominate. When you learn to swim, you could spend a lot of the time learning strokes out of the water, but the only way to really learn to swim is by swimming. Similarly, in prayer and meditation, you can spend a lot of time on techniques trying to know about God, but the real point of it is to know God.

We need to realize that God is much closer than we think and to recognize when we have arrived in the presence of God. When you arrive in God's presence you often experience a kind of serenity and have pleasurable sensations. These are called the "consolations of God." God uses these consolations to lure us, to bribe us into wanting to be with Him. They are like sweets we use to reward children. As our relationship with God matures, we often no longer experience these sweets when we pray. God reckons that we are no longer childish nor need to be bribed in this way. Just as we give a child the food the child needs, first feeding her milk after she is born but eventually giving her more substantial fare, so God gives us more substantial fare as we mature in our spiritual life. God wants us to love God for who He is, not for what we can get out of Him.

There comes a time when we evolve, we grow, and we realize that all that actually matters in prayer is being with our Beloved, being with God. Just being together, just like when we're together with the one we love, holding hands and savoring being together with them. Words give way; they are almost superfluous and totally inadequate. Just as if we were to describe a sunrise or the birth of a child, the most eloquent thing is silence. We don't always need to be talking with the one we love. Sitting there in silence or listening to music is almost indescribably satisfying and sweet. That is what it's like to be with God in these times of satisfaction and joy.

We arrive and yet the journey continues, as we grow ever more in our God awareness. This God awareness is shown by our God likeness, and how we are increasingly becoming what we love. People tend to look like the things they love—which is why so many people end up looking like their dogs! But we can also look like God if we love God and strive to be like God.

ABOVE: READING THE KORAN AT THE TOMB OF THE
PROPHET HUD IN HADHRAMAUT, SOUTH YEMEN.
OPPOSITE: AN IRISH CATHOLIC ATTENDS AN
OPEN-AIR MASS ON GARLAND SUNDAY.
FOLLOWING PAGES: DEMONSTRATORS RAISE
HANDS IN PRAYER AT A GATHERING AGAINST
VIOLENCE IN RIO DE JANEIRO, BRAZIL.

Voice of the Rising Tide .... Thich Nhat Hanh

When your mind is liberated your heart floods with compassion: compassion for yourself, for having undergone countless sufferings because you were not yet able to relieve yourself of false views, hatred, ignorance, and anger; and compassion for others because they do not yet see and so are still imprisoned by false views, hatred, and ignorance and continue to create suffering for themselves and for others. Now you look at yourself and at others with the eyes of compassion, like a saint who hears the cry of every creature in the universe and whose voice is the voice of every person who has seen reality in perfect wholeness. As a Buddhist Sutra hears the voice of the Bodhisattva of compassion:

> *The wondrous voice, the voice of the one*
> > *who attends to the cries of the world*
> *The noble voice, the voice of the rising tide*
> > *surpassing all the sounds of the world*
> *Let our mind be attuned to that voice.*
> *Put aside all doubt and meditate on the pure*
> > *and holy nature of the regarder of the cries of the world*
> *Because that is our reliance in situations of*
> > *pain, distress, calamity, death.*
> *Perfect in all merits, beholding all sentient*
> > *beings with compassionate eyes, making the ocean of blessings limitless,*
> *Before this one, we should incline.*

Practice looking at all beings with the eyes of compassion: this is the meditation called "the meditation on compassion."

The meditation on compassion must be realized during the hours you sit and during every moment you carry out service for others. No matter where you go or where you sit, remember the sacred call: "Look at all beings with the eyes of compassion."

There are many subjects and methods for meditation, so many that I could never hope to write them all down for our friends. I've only mentioned a few, simple but basic methods here. A peace worker is like any one else. She or he must live her own life. Work is only a part of life. But work is life only when done in mindfulness. Otherwise, one becomes like the person "who lives as though dead." We need to light our own torch in order to carry on. But the life of each one of us is connected with the life of those around us. If we know how to live in mindfulness, if we know how to preserve and care for our own mind and heart, then thanks to that, our brothers and sisters will also know how to live in mindfulness ...

treated more carefully than anything else. In mindfulness, compassion, irritation, mustard green plant, and teapot are all sacred.

Sitting in mindfulness, both our bodies and minds can be at peace and totally relaxed. But this state of peace and relaxation differs fundamentally from the lazy, semi-conscious state of mind that one gets while resting and dozing. Sitting in such lazy semi-consciousness, far from being mindfulness, is like sitting in a dark cave. In mindfulness one is not only restful and happy, but alert and awake. Meditation is not evasion; it is a serene encounter with reality. The person who practices mindfulness should be no less awake than the driver of a car; if the practitioner isn't awake he will be possessed by dispersion and forgetfulness, just as the drowsy driver is likely to cause a grave accident. But as awake as a person walking on high stilts—any misstep could cause the walker to fall. Be like a medieval knight walking weaponless in a forest of swords. Be like a lion, going forward with slow, gentle, and firm steps. Only with this kind of vigilance can you realize total awakening.

For beginners, I recommend the method of pure recognition: recognition without judgment. Feelings, whether of compassion or irritation, should be welcomed, recognized, and treated on an absolutely equal basis; because both are ourselves. The tangerine I am eating is me. The mustard greens I am planting are me. I plant with all my heart and mind. I clean this teapot with the kind of attention I would have were I giving the baby Buddha or Jesus a bath. Nothing should be

When possessed by a sadness, an anxiety, a hatred, or a passion or whatever, the method of pure observation and recognition may seem difficult to practice. If so, turn to meditation on a fixed object, using your own state of mind as meditation's subject. Such meditation reveals and heals. The sadness or anxiety, hatred or passion, under the gaze of concentration and meditation reveals its own nature—a revelation that leads naturally to healing and emancipation. The sadness (or whatever has caused the pain) can be used as a means of liberation from torment and suffering, like using a thorn to remove a thorn. We should treat our anxiety, our pain, our hatred and passion gently, respectfully, not resisting it, but living with it, making peace with it, penetrating into its nature by meditation on interdependence. One quickly learns how to select subjects of meditation that fit the situation. Subjects of meditation—like interdependence, compassion, self, emptiness, non-attachment—all these belong to the categories of meditation which have the power to reveal and to heal.

Meditation on these subjects, however, can only be successful if we have built up a certain power of concentration, a power achieved by the practice of mindfulness in everyday life, in the observation and recognition of all that is going on. But the objects of meditation must be realities that have real roots in yourselves—not just subjects of philosophical speculation. Each should be like a kind of food that must be cooked for a long time over a hot fire. We put it in a pot, cover it, and light the fire. The pot is ourselves and the heat used to cook is the power of concentration. The fuel comes from the continuous practice of mindfulness. Without enough heat the food will never be cooked. But once cooked, the food reveals its true nature and helps lead us to liberation.

ABOVE: DRESSED IN PRAYER ROBES, A
MUSLIM GIRL AND HER MOTHER SAVOR THE
SERENITY OF THE BAITURRAHMAN GREAT
MOSQUE IN BANDA ACEH, INDONESIA.
OPPOSITE: A BUDDHIST MONK IN BHUTAN
RINGS A PRAYER BELL.
FOLLOWING PAGES: QERO INDIANS PRAY AT
A WAYSIDE SHRINE IN MOUNTAINOUS CUZCO
PROVINCE, PERU.

Reaching Out

PRAYER STRENGTHENS THE BONDS OF COMMUNITY AND COMPASSION

Prayer .... Kathleen Norris

Prayer was impossible for me for years. For a time I was so alienated from my religious heritage that I had the vainglorious notion that somehow, if I prayed, I would cause more harm than good. But when a priest I knew asked me to pray for him—he'd been diagnosed with a serious illness—my "yes" was immediate, sincere, and complete. I wasn't sure that I could pray well and was shocked that the priest would trust me to do so. But I recognized that this was my pride speaking, the old perfectionism that has dogged me since I was a child. Well, or badly, that was beside the point. Of course I could pray, and I did.

The ancient monks understood that a life of prayer would manifest itself in relationships with others. "If prayer is a matter of concern to you," said the sixth-century monk John Climacus, "then show yourself to be merciful." As "a dialog and a union with God," he said, "prayer has the effect of [holding] the world together." This seems a radical perception of prayer, running counter to the understanding of prayer that prevailed in Protestant seminaries during the 1960s and 1970s. Clergy have told me that during those years even to mention that one prayed could be dangerous, inviting a lecture from a professor or another student on the dangers of pietism. As one minister told me, echoing comments I had heard from many others, "The emphasis was all on the social gospel, on applying religion to society's problems, and to talk about your own spiritual life, your practice of prayer, was extremely suspect." This attitude, which apparently was held as orthodoxy in some circles, may help explain why so many Protestants, including pastors, began showing up at monasteries during the 1980s, asking for spiritual direction and a chance to recover the tradition of prayer. More and more of us, it seems, share Thomas Merton's belief, as he once stated it in a letter to Daniel Berrigan, written during the turmoil of the 1960s, that "there is an absolute need for the solitary, bare, dark . . . kind of prayer . . . Unless that dimension is there in the Church somewhere the whole caboodle lacks life and light and intelligence too. It is a kind of hidden, secret, unknown stabilizer, and a compass too."

Benedictines know that their personal and communal prayer need to be in balance; one affects the other, and the whole provides the support that they need to remain faithful in their

LEFT: GANGES RIVER, VARANASI, INDIA. PREVIOUS PAGES: EASTER VIGIL AT ST. GREGORY NYSSEN EPISCOPAL CHURCH IN SAN FRANCISCO, CALIFORNIA.

response to the monastic call. I suspect that many members of ordinary church congregations would say much the same thing about the way that their own everyday prayer is reflected in the experience of Sunday worship and vice versa. While prayer may originate in our own desires, it quickly moves beyond them, into our life with others, and toward the greater society. The inward/outward dynamic of prayer is perfectly expressed in the way that the sixth-century monk Dorotheus of Gaza imagined our world. He saw it as a circle, with God at the center and our lives as lines drawn from the circumference toward the center. As Dorotheus relates it, the closer the lines crowd in toward God, "the closer they are to one another; and the closer they are to one another, the closer they become to God."

Dorotheus demonstrates the kind of wisdom I have come to expect from serious and habitual practitioners of prayer. They have moved way beyond the simplistic "gimme, gimme" of pietistic or privatized prayer, which can function as a kind of Republican agenda for the soul: Give me mine, and let those less worthy fend for themselves. Grounding themselves in a profound, all-encompassing gratitude for all that God has given them, including their trials and tribulations, they are open to both the private and the public dimensions of prayer. Their prayer is not pie-in-the-sky, but stark realism. I think of a local priest, Fr. Tom Gorman, who having been diagnosed with a terminal illness, collapsed on Ash Wednesday and died during Lent, refusing his bishop's offer to allow him to return home. "I want to stay with my parish," he had said, turning his own suffering and death into a prayer, the kind of presence that touched everyone in the church, and in the town.

Sometimes people will say things like, "Your prayers didn't work, but thanks," as if a person could be praying for only one thing. A miracle. A cure. But in the hardest situations, all one can do is to ask for God's mercy: Let my friend die at home, Lord, and not in the hospital. Let her go quickly, God, and with her loved ones present. One Benedictine friend, a gentle, thoughtful man who has been in constant physical pain for years and is now confined to a wheelchair, says of prayer, "Often, all I can do is to ask God, 'Lord, what is it you want of me?'" From him I have learned that prayer is not asking for what you think you want but asking to be changed in ways you can't imagine. To be made more grateful, more able to see the good in what you have been given instead of always grieving for what might have been. People who are in the habit of praying—and they include the mystics of the Christian tradition—know that when a prayer is answered, it is never in a way that you expect.

But prayer stumbles over modern self-consciousness and self-reliance, a remarkably ingenuous belief in our ability to set goals and attain them as quickly as possible. I recently received a mailing from a group of New Age witches who state, in a kind of creed, their belief that "I can create my own reality and that sending out a positive expectation will bring a positive result." I suspect that only America could have produced Pollyanna witches, part and parcel of our pragmatism, our addiction to self-help and "how-to." No wonder we have difficulty with prayer, for which the best "how-to" I know is from Psalm 46: "be still and know that I am God" (v. 11, Grail). This can happen in an instant; it can also constitute a life's work.

ABOVE: A PRIEST BLESSES A GROUP OF
YOUNG SAAMI MEN IN KAUTOKEINO, NORWAY.

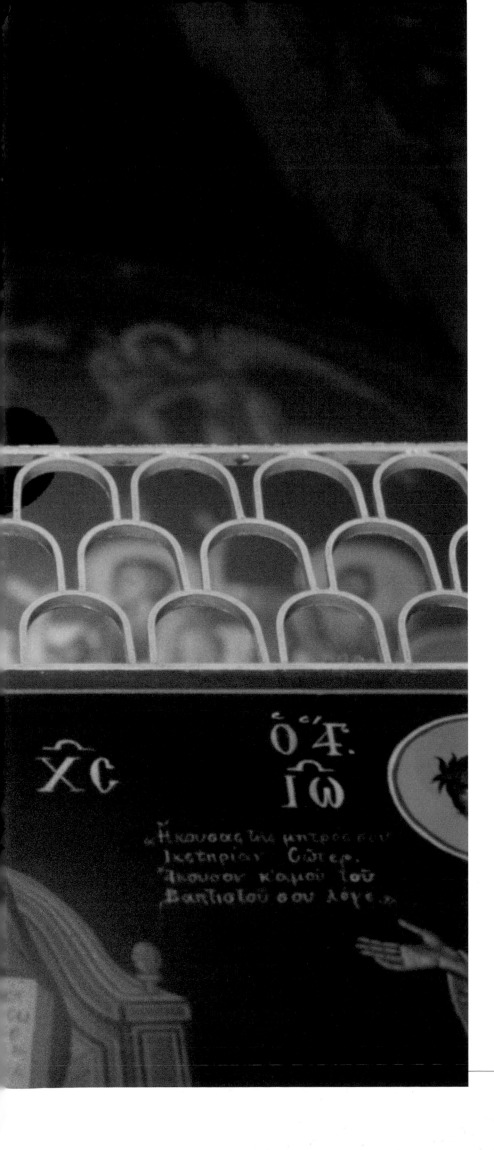

EASTER MASS IN LEVADIA, GREECE.

The Portable Doorway .... Michael Wolfe

People the world over pray to God, but they don't all speak in the same way. Even the words we use to describe the act are different. The Latin root for prayer, which conditions our view, is an active verb, *precor,* to ask, to beseech, to implore. The word implies desire and fulfillment. By contrast, the conventional Muslim prayer, called *al-Salat,* is related to an Aramaic root meaning to bow, to bend, to stretch, a reference to the series of postures—bowing, kneeling, touching the forehead to the ground—that Muslims perform while reciting verses of praise and supplication, mostly from the Koran. But salat is more than an act, it is a condition. The great Muslim poet Jalaluddin Rumi wrote, "There is no salat without the presence of the heart." This heart-presence is the state of salat.

Muslims perform salat several times a day, at intervals prescribed by the angle of the sun. Its performance is common throughout the Muslim world, part and parcel of work-a-day society, a sanctified, but not a rare or rarefied event. Riding in a taxicab in Cairo or Karachi, your driver may pull over, grab a prayer rug from the trunk, and pause en route for his devotions. Business people in corporate boardrooms, students in libraries, athletes at the gym, people in all walks of life observe these time-outs at the appointed hours. It is a second, spiritual clock by which whole societies keep time.

In Islam, one is called to prayer. This insistence on the invitation to pray has inspired the building of thousands of minarets that are Islam's landmark symbol around the world. The voice that calls from these towers proclaims God's oneness. It beckons people to prosperity, to spiritual success through an act of humbling devotion. The call reminds Muslims that God is great and worth the effort of communication.

This dialog is the essence of salat: a few quiet minutes carved out of one's day to communicate with the source of existence. No priest is required, no intermediary. The conversation is between the communicant and the Creator, and it is assumed that God will answer, not simply in words but in world events.

Generally speaking, salat is not a time to pray for oneself. There is a short place toward the very end of the Sunni version where one may petition God, but most people take this

"You must make the connection between prayer and life. The closer you are to the heart of God, the closer you come to the heart of the world, the closer you come to others."

Henri J.M. Nouwen

to mean a chance to call down well-being on oneself, one's family, friends and teachers, and the lineage of the prophets from Abraham to Muhammad. The emotional core of salat is not self-fulfillment but a ritual *cri de coeur* for guidance, an expression of gratefulness for divine compassion, and a reminder of God's unity.

The distance between God and man is often emphasized, even romanticized, in Western literature, sometimes with great irony and beauty as when the American poet Theodore Roethke cries out to God, "From me to Thee's a long and terrible way!" Such anguished separation stands in stark contrast to an idea expressed in the Koran that God is as near to you as the veins in your neck. That nearness may be experienced as a comfort but also as an ethical imperative: behave well, for God is always near. God's proximity gives salat a special meaning, as a dialogue with one's divine interiority.

Prior to salat, Muslims are instructed to perform a ritual washing of the hands, arms, face, and feet. Salat is sometimes described as a kind of cleansing, too. Muhammad once likened it to a stream running by one's house; he recommended stepping into it five times a day. Muslim prayer is a step into another element—out of the material realm, into what some mystics call the Unseen World.

Such mystical notions are often discounted in our rational age, though few would disagree that ideas, feelings, desires, and fears—all intangible—are the engines that drive the reality we inhabit. God is invisible too, although the Koran remarks that for "thinking people" evidence of his presence is all around us: "Look around!— In the creation of sky and land; in sailing ships that cross the sea for mankind's profit; in waters sent down from the sky and the life He gives to land that appears extinguished; in living creatures of all kinds and the way they multiply, in the changing winds and the clouds that follow them between the sky and earth, everywhere there are signs for reflective people." Salat is a means of attuning one's attention to these signs, in nature and in human affairs. It is a portable doorway into a realm of heightened awareness.

By portable, I mean that one may perform salat anywhere, on any patch of clean or covered ground. Mosques are hallowed spaces, but, as Muhammad pointed out, the whole earth is a mosque at times of prayer. Though praying among others comes highly recommended, Muslims hold that each man and woman has, through salat, direct access to the Divine without intercessors. Prayer is a conversation between earth and heaven, created and Creator, the seen and the Unseen.

Performing salat in a group lends a collective energy to the experience. Joining dozens or even hundreds of fellow Muslims in synchronized motion creates the sensation of being connected to something larger—history, community, tradition. Ordinary Muslims don't much concern themselves with theological proofs of God's existence. Ask a Muslim and he will tell you that God is in the hearts of the believers. In this sense, gatherings of people engaged in communal prayer magnify God's presence.

The sensation is unmistakable during the holy month of Ramadan, when devout Muslims fast from sunrise to sunset. Attending a mosque in the evening feels like joining a small village. Dinner is often served. Additional prayers accompany salat. Many people stay on after the service to hear a portion of the Koran recited, usually by one of the group's more gifted Arabic speakers. Like Gregorian cantillation, the entwining of rhythm and meaning is verbal music, even for those of us who have no real facility for the language. Many Muslims say that a few minutes of well-chanted Koran has the power to induce a state of heightened consciousness.

The frisson of communal prayer is all the more intense during the Hajj, the annual pilgrimage to Mecca that Muslims are encouraged to undertake at least once in a lifetime. During the Hajj, when as many as a million people descend upon the mosque at Mecca, the door of salat swings wide open, giving the impression that one is praying with the whole world.

My first view of this scene was in a poster, shot with a wide-angle lens from a nearby peak. The photo showed a courtyard filled with pilgrims waiting to perform salat. At the center of the courtyard stood the Ka'bah, Mecca's signature black-draped shrine, with a few thousand people walking around it. Twenty years ago I pinned this poster to a wall in my California home, as I was starting to teach myself salat. The learning process took months; the photo helped. It was shot at night in time-lapse, so that the people surrounding the Ka'bah were at once recognizable individuals but fused together in a swirl of white robes. A friend said the rings of pilgrims, viewed from so high up, resembled the blow-up of a thumbprint. She thought for a moment, then added, God's thumbprint.

When I finally arrived in Mecca a few years later, I walked straight to the mosque. It was eleven o'clock in the morning, the building was filling up for the noon prayer, and the streets flowed with white-robed men and women. The Meccan mosque rests in a hollow at the lowest point in town. The crowd moved toward it slowly, everyone trending downward like honey from a bottle.

About an hour later, the last call to prayer rang from the minarets. I was still a hundred yards from the entrance. I didn't pray inside the mosque that day. It was Friday, and the turnout filled the building quickly. I performed salat on the street, and I wasn't alone. Fifty thousand of us filled the hollow standing shoulder to shoulder.

Later that day, when the crowds had thinned, I rode an escalator to the rooftop. Viewed from the roof, the Ka'bah looked like a rock dropped into a pond, the people around it moving in ripples. From such a height, it was easy to appreciate the choreography of a mass salat as Muslims from every corner of the world bowed and rose up together, drawn by a desire to communicate with the divine presence that resides within themselves and connects them to all humanity.

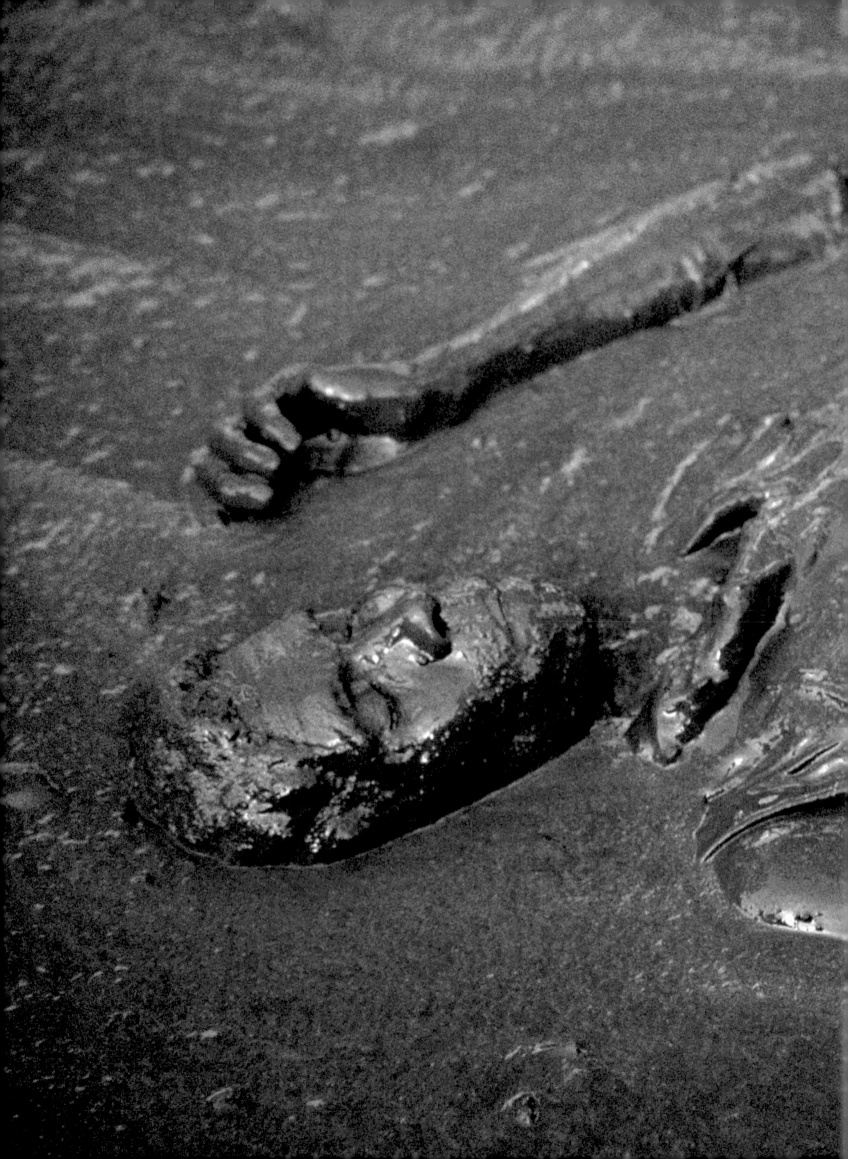

ABOVE: DOUSED IN SACRED CORNMEAL AND
EARTH, AN APACHE GIRL PRAYS FOR THE GOOD
OF HER PEOPLE DURING A FOUR-DAY INITIATION
RITE KNOWN AS THE SUNRISE CEREMONY.
PREVIOUS PAGES: A VOODOO DEVOTEE IMMERSED
IN A MUD POOL AT PLAINE DU NORD IN HAITI
COMMUNES WITH THE WARRIOR SPIRIT OGOU.

Beauty is before me

And beauty is behind me

Above and below me hovers the beautiful

I am surrounded by it

I am immersed in it

In my youth I am aware of it

And in old age I shall walk quietly

The beautiful trail.

—*Navajo Blessing Way*

Lectio Divina .... Kathleen Norris

"Lectio Divina" literally means "holy reading," and would not have been a scary word for me had my first encounters with it in monastic literature not made it sound like an esoteric practice that I could never hope to employ. The classic definitions of contemplative reading have their uses, but when I was just starting out as a Benedictine oblate, I found their talk of stages, and attaining ever-more profound levels of meaning, thoroughly discouraging. It was as if I would have to evolve into a higher life form—or at least one with more patience and a longer attention span—in order to attempt lectio at all.

When I finally confessed my misgivings to the monk who was the abbey's oblate director, he informed me that as far as he was concerned, I was already doing lectio. He had found the practice evident in the poetry I was writing in response to the scriptures I encountered in the monastery's liturgy of the hours. His words lifted a burden from me, as I had become aware that the venerable practice of lectio is one of the core experiences of Benedictine life. He helped me to understand that it is a daily meditation on scripture in which one reads not for knowledge or information but to enhance one's life of faith. Thus, it is not a method but rather a type of freeform, serious play. One might read a passage aloud, trying on different voices: Pilate's "What is truth?" as a sarcastic aside not requiring a response, or as a brief moment of wonder, inviting a response that does not come. One might attempt to memorize a verse or two of scripture and let it percolate through the consciousness while going about one's work, allowing the words to become a part of everyday life, illuminating one's relationships with others, and with the self.

The juxtapositions can be startling—once, on my birthday, I encountered the stern admonition of Deuteronomy 32:18: "You were unmindful of the Rock that bore you; you forgot the God who gave you birth." This slap on the face caused me to reflect on my great capacity for distraction, for mind-numbing unmindfulness of God's presence. But it was also a powerful reminder of the fact that my birthday is not mine alone but celebrates the willingness of my mother to undergo a pregnancy and labor. It is a mark of God's work in the lives of my mother and father, and their mothers and fathers before them. The mundane stuff of inheritance, but also a mystery.

READING SCRIPTURE
AT THE WESTERN
WALL IN JERUSALEM.

"The important thing is not the finding, it is the seeking, it is the devotion with which one spins the wheel of prayer and scripture, discovering the truth little by little."

Ursula K. LeGuin

A MUSLIM WORSHIPER READS THE KORAN IN A SINGAPORE MOSQUE.

Lectio can suddenly place you in a Bible story, as happened to me in a monastery one day when I was reading the day's gospel text in preparation for Mass, and saw myself in the desperate father in the ninth chapter of Mark who has brought his son to Jesus to be healed of demons. As one does when someone is drastically ill, the father recounts the history of the disease. And then he asks Jesus to have pity and help him. My husband's medical and psychological difficulties had been acute; he was at the time contending with both depression and recovery from serious abdominal surgery. I began to read the scripture passage as if I was at the monastery for David's sake, to ask Jesus for help with his sickness of body and spirit. But as that father came to realize, I was also there for myself, to hear the words that Jesus speaks: "All things can be done for the one who believes," and also to respond from the heart, "Lord, I believe; help my unbelief!" (Mark 9:23-24).

Recently, at a conference devoted to the subject of the Benedictine use of scripture, it became clear to me that for monastic people lectio divina is not so much a technique of reading as a way of life. It is the freedom to ask anything of scripture without requiring an answer or expecting to reach a conclusion, let alone to fit the scripture into one's preconceptions. It is asking in a spirit that is opposed to the spirit of inquisition. When a lecturer invited us to employ the non-methods of lectio with Psalm 1, which begins: "Happy indeed are those/who follow not the counsel of the wicked . . . " (Grail), questions quickly began to fly around the room: Is this the prayer of a self-righteous person? If it's a prayer, why are none of the lines addressed to God? Who are the wicked? Does God watch over only the just? One nun found the psalm to be a vivid depiction of fundamental choices, comparable to the passage in Deuteronomy in which life and death are set before Israel, and the people are asked to choose life. As the conversation continued, I was struck by its openness and daring. These are people who practice Bible reading as part of their ascetic discipline, daring to grapple with the hardest, most difficult texts of scripture. And it has made them both bold and free.

We dwelt a good long while with the image of the just person as a "tree that is planted/beside the flowing waters,/that yields its fruit in due season/and whose leaves shall never fade" (v.3, Grail). Several told stories of people in their own lives who had been models of such abundant goodness, whose gifts did not fade as they aged, or even after they had died. We played with the image of trees in the context of the entire Bible, one person seeing in Psalm 1 the tree of the knowledge of good and evil from the book of Genesis, another finding the tree of life in the Revelation to John. And we happily discussed many of the biblical trees in between: the oaks of Mamre, Daniel's use of trees to bring Susanna justice after she is falsely accused of adultery, Jonah's sorry little gourd tree, the tree of Jesse foretold in Isaiah that appears each year in Advent and Christmas carols, the image of Jesus as a vine in John 15, and, of course, the tree on which Jesus died.

A SERBIAN ORTHODOX PRIEST STUDIES
SCRIPTURE AT A BELGRADE MONASTERY.

When our group turned to Psalm 82, which begins: "God stands in the divine assembly,/and gives judgment in the midst of the gods ..." (Grail), the questions raised demonstrated the way in which lectio can turn away from the reader and toward the world. Is the psalm a warning to the powers that be in any age? Is it an attack on personal and collective idolatries? Who are "the afflicted and the needy" (v.3, Grail)? Does the psalm describe the end of the world, or does it depict holy patience, God's willingness to warn us away from our unjust judgments? Is the psalm a prophesy or a lament? Or is it an exorcism, a doing away with injustice? A giddy democracy surfaced in the room; a Hebrew translator remarked on the literal meaning of a word, followed by a person with no scholarly sophistication who added a bit of spiritual insight that could only have come from a lifetime of praying over the passage. The knowledge of scripture reflected in the group, ranging from young monastics with doctorates from Claremont, Oxford, and the Biblicum in Rome, to older monks and nuns whose reading of the Bible has been primarily devotional, mirrored the diversity that might be found in any monastery. (Or, for that matter, in church congregations.) St. Benedict, writing in the sixth century, expected that many of the monks would be illiterate; the practice of lectio he outlined for them consisted of memorizing large portions of scripture, beginning with the psalms. As a practice of prayer, lectio is open to anyone.

Although most Benedictines these days read and write, they still value knowing scripture "by heart" as a spiritual discipline. One nun, a scholar, described the process of lectio as bringing her whole self to the text. "Anything I can learn from anywhere can be helpful," she said, admitting that she does her lectio in Hebrew with the Old Testament and in Greek with the New. But, she added, "it's not because I can, but because it slows me down," forcing her to engage with each word, and not simply reading quickly to cover the material. "Even though I teach the modern methods of biblical interpretation," she said, "I find that for the purpose of lectio they're limited and I can't stay in them. It's as if lectio divina is my native tongue, and as a Benedictine, I keep returning there."

Although Benedictines practice lectio privately, they are well aware of its communal dimension, and the way that lectio can instruct a person who wishes to take the Bible personally without privatizing it. Reading the story of Mary and Martha in Luke 10, for example, I can easily find myself in both women. I can hear Martha muttering, her housewife's meter running, as she is so overcome with the work of hospitality—the cleaning to be done, the food to be prepared and served—that she risks becoming inhospitable. She's my Type-A side, rushing to get the job done but at too great a cost.

Mary is pure Type-B, the procrastinator and dreamer, the person who knows that no small part of welcoming a guest is the ability to settle down and listen. She is my better self, the one I have to strive for. As I continue to ponder the story, I begin to see it as a portrait of my mar-

riage, my husband's procrastinating wisdom bouncing off my "getting-it-done" wisdom, each of us in the right only as we are willing to value and learn from the other. I meditate more on Mary's silence, because I know Martha's all too well.

Martha may do her work in silence, but it is a sham, a mask for rage. I like to think of her as saying nothing as she bangs around the house, trying to get Mary's attention, or better yet, make her feel guilty for not helping out. At any rate, Martha is so internally noisy that Jesus has to call her by name twice—"Martha, Martha"—before she can hear him and respond. I recognize myself all too clearly in that scene; all the internal—infernal—distractions, the clatter-bang of daily routines and deadlines, that can make me unfit company for anyone.

And this leads me to consider the nature of Mary's silence, which is the gift of being able to sit at God's feet and listen. It is not silence as enforced by the world, the false silence that an adult seeks to impose on a child, for example, in an abusive relationship. It is not the silence of the story that a browbeaten woman might have told, were it not for social and economic pressures bent on keeping her quiet. It is not the silence of the writer jailed for exposing a lie, or of the political prisoner, whose silence is often bought with blood. It is a good, healthy, open silence, a freeing silence that might lead a person anywhere. Even to lectio, to a reading of the Bible that is free to question it, and also to let it question you. Jesus' role in the process is to name it, to call it "the better part" (Luke 10:42).

All of this meandering through the text, and my personal reflection on it, does not remain private if I employ it in a sermon to help others find themselves in the story, or even if I use it to remind myself to be more charitable to the Marthas and the Marys that I meet. It is this dimension of scripture that keeps drawing me back to the process of lectio and allows me to enjoy the surprising God I find there, God as ultimate, inexhaustible poet, giving me in mere words much more than I could have imagined. For many years I never looked at a Bible; now I find that it sustains me in ways no poem or novel could. I find no easy answers in the Bible, but only a holy simplicity. Paul's insight, for example, that "love never ends" (I Cor. 13:8), asks me to recognize that love sometimes comes as judgment, holding me accountable for what I do. Like an exasperating but invaluable friend, the Bible keeps bringing me back to my senses, often in bracing (and comical) ways. Not long ago, I had an especially difficult writing assignment, with a tight deadline. I had pages of notes from interviews and my own reading to assemble—an experience that always brings to mind Emily Dickinson's poignant remark regarding herself: "When I try to organize, my little Force explodes." After much exploding, a marathon session of writing, a period of revising that became indistinguishable from insomnia, then printing out, pondering, and more revising, I finally got a draft into the mail. Exhausted, but with a considerable feeling of accomplishment, I sat down to read the gospel for the day. Lectio found me, if you will, in a paraphrase of Luke 17:10: Unprofitable servant, you have only done what was required of you. I could only laugh. But when a week later the essay was summarily rejected with a "sorry, we can't use it," I felt as if I had run into a brick wall at ninety miles per hour. Recalling this Bible verse was a great help; it set me free to accept the situation with a minimum of fuss, and move on.

Meditating on Compassion .... The Dalai Lama

If we truly intend to develop compassion, we have to devote more time to it than our formal meditation sessions grant us. It is a goal we must commit ourselves to with all our heart. If we do have a time each day when we like to sit and contemplate, that is very good. As I have suggested, early mornings are a good time for such contemplation, since our minds are particularly clear then. We must, however, devote more than just this period to cultivating compassion. During our more formal sessions, for example, we work at developing empathy and closeness to others. We reflect upon their miserable predicament. And once we have generated a true feeling of compassion within ourselves, we should hold on to it, simply experience it, using the settled meditation I have described to remain focused, without applying thought or reason. This enables it to sink in. And when the feeling begins to weaken, we again apply reasons to restimulate our compassion. We go between these two methods of meditation, much as potters work their clay, moistening it and then forming it as they see the need.

It is generally best that we initially not spend too much time in formal meditation. We shall not generate compassion for all beings overnight. We won't succeed in a month or a year. If we are able to diminish our selfish instincts and develop a little more concern for others before our death, we have made good use of this life. If, instead, we push ourselves to attain Buddhahood in a short time, we'll soon grow tired of our practice. The mere sight of the seat where we engage in our formal morning meditation will stimulate resistance ...

It is said that the ultimate state of Buddhahood is attainable within a human lifetime. This is for extraordinary practitioners who have devoted many previous lives to preparing themselves for this opportunity. We can feel only admiration for such beings and use their example to develop perseverance instead of pushing ourselves to any extreme. It is best to pursue a middle path between lethargy and fanaticism.

We should ensure that whatever we do, we maintain some effect or influence from our meditation so that it directs our actions as we live our everyday lives. By our doing so, everything we do outside our formal sessions becomes part of our training in compassion. It is not difficult for us to develop sympathy for a child in the hospital or an acquaintance mourning the death of a spouse. We must start to consider how to keep our hearts open toward those we would normally envy, those who enjoy fine lifestyles and wealth. With an ever deeper recognition of what suffering is, gained from our meditation sessions, we become able to relate to such people with compassion. Eventually we should be able to relate to all beings this way, seeing that their situation is always dependent upon the conditions of the vicious cycle of life. In this way all interactions with others become catalysts for deepening our compassion. This is how we keep our hearts open in our daily lives, outside of our formal meditation periods.

True compassion has the intensity and spontaneity of a loving mother caring for her suffering baby. Throughout the day, such a mother's concern for her child affects all her thoughts and actions. This is the attitude we are working to cultivate toward each and every being. When we experience this, we have generated "great compassion."

Once one has become profoundly moved by great compassion and loving-kindness, and had one's heart stirred by altruistic thoughts, one must pledge to devote oneself to freeing all beings from the suffering they endure within cyclic existence, the vicious circle of birth, death, and rebirth we are all prisoners of. Our suffering is not limited to our present situation. According to the Buddhist view, our present situation as humans is relatively comfortable. However, we stand to experience much difficulty in the future if we misuse this present opportunity. Compassion enables us to refrain from thinking in a self-centered way. We experience great joy and never fall to the extreme of simply seeking our own personal happiness and salvation. We continually strive to develop and perfect our virtue and wisdom. With such compassion, we shall eventually possess all the necessary conditions for attaining enlightenment. We must therefore cultivate compassion from the very start of our spiritual practice.

ABOVE: TIBETAN BUDDHISTS GATHER FOR THE
DALAI LAMA'S TEACHINGS IN SARNATH, INDIA.
FOLLOWING PAGES: COPTIC MONASTERY, EGYPT.

Contributors and Credits

Writers

Karen Armstrong is a prominent scholar of religious affairs. She is the author of several best-selling books, including *The Battle for God*, *The History of God*, and *Through the Narrow Gate*, a memoir of her seven years as a Catholic nun.

His Holiness the Dalai Lama is the spiritual leader of Tibetan Buddhists and Tibet's political leader-in-exile. His many books include *An Open Heart*, *The Art of Happiness*, and *Freedom in Exile*. Awarded the Nobel Peace Prize in 1989, His Holiness is recognized as one of the world's preeminent spiritual leaders.

Mohandas K. Gandhi led India's movement for independence from Great Britain. His practice of nonviolent protest has influenced struggles for civil rights and independence worldwide.

Zen master and peace activist **Thich Nhat Hanh** was nominated for the Nobel Prize by Dr. Martin Luther King, Jr., in 1967. His books include *Peace Is Every Step*, *Living Buddha, Living Christ*, *The Miracle of Mindfulness*, and *The Energy of Prayer.*

Jack Kornfield was trained as a Buddhist monk in Thailand, Burma, and India and is a co-founder of the Insight Meditation Society and Spirit Rock Center. His books include *A Path with Heart*, *Seeking the Heart of Wisdom*, and *After the Ecstasy, the Laundry.*

Rabbi Harold Kushner is the best-selling author of *When Bad Things Happen to Good People* and *Living a Life That Matters.*

Regarded as one of the most influential Christian thinkers of the 20th century, **C. S. Lewis** was the author of a wide range of books, including the beloved children's series *The Chronicles of Narnia* and such religion titles as *Mere Christianity*, *Christian Reflections*, and *The Screwtape Letters.*

Thomas Merton, who became a Trappist monk in the Cistercian Abbey of Gethsemani in Kentucky, was the author of more than 40 books, including *New Seeds of Contemplation*, *No Man Is an Island*, and *The Seven Storey Mountain*. He is acknowledged as one of the foremost spiritual thinkers of the 20th century.

Thomas Moore is a former Catholic monk and author of the best-selling *Care of the Soul* and *The Soul's Religion.*

Seyyed Hossein Nasr, an expert on Islamic science and spirituality, is University Professor of Islamic Studies at George Washington University. Professor Nasr is the author of numerous books, including

Man and Nature: The Spiritual Crisis in Modern Man, *Religion and the Order of Nature*, and *Knowledge and the Sacred.*

Kathleen Norris is the author of *Dakota: A Spiritual Geography*, *The Cloister Walk*, and *Amazing Grace: A Vocabulary of Faith.*

John Paul II, born Karol Józef Wojtyła, was elected Pope in 1978. His pontificate lasted nearly 27 years, one of the longest and most influential in the history of the Church.

Huston Smith is Professor of Religion and Distinguished Adjunct Professor of Philosophy, Emeritus, at Syracuse University. Holder of twelve honorary degrees, his many books include *The World's Religions*, which has sold more than 2½ million copies, and *Why Religion Matters*, which won the 2002 Wilbur Award for the best book on religion. In 1996 Bill Moyers devoted a PBS special, "The Wisdom of Faith with Huston Smith," to his life and work.

David Steindl-Rast is a Benedictine monk and advocate of contemplative prayer. He is the author of numerous books, including *A Listening Heart*, *Gratefulness: The Heart of Prayer*, and *Music of Silence*. Brother David serves a worldwide Network for Grateful Living through www.gratefulness.org.

Phyllis Tickle is the former Contributing Editor in Religion to *Publishers Weekly* and author of some two dozen books, including *God-Talk in America*, *Prayer Is a Place: America's Spiritual Landscape Observed*, and *The Divine Hours* trilogy.

Desmond Tutu is the former Archbishop of Cape Town, South Africa, and recipient of the 1984 Nobel Peace Prize. Collections of his speeches, sermons, and other writings include *Crying in the Wilderness*, *The Rainbow People of God*, and *God Has a Dream.*

Awarded the Nobel Peace Prize in 1986, **Elie Wiesel** is the author of more than forty books, including *Against Silence*, *Souls on Fire*, and the Holocaust memoir *Night*. He is the founder, with his wife Marion, of The Elie Wiesel Foundation for Humanity.

Michael Wolfe is an author and film producer. His books include *The Hadj*, *One Thousand Roads to Mecca*, and *Taking Back Islam*. His film *Muhammad: Legacy of a Prophet* was broadcast on PBS in 2002. He is a columnist for Beliefnet.com.

Carol Zaleski is Professor of Religion at Smith College in Northampton, Massachusetts, and co-author of *Prayer: A History.*

PHOTOGRAPHERS

Acclaimed photographer **Abbas** is a member of the Magnum Agency in Paris, where he now lives. His books include *Allah O Akbar* and *Faces of Christianity.*

James L. Amos was a photographer with the National Geographic Society for twenty-six years. He was twice named Magazine Photographer of the Year by the National Press Photographers Association and received many awards from the White House News Photographers Association.

Peter Armenia is a travel photographer based in Durham, North Carolina. His work has been published in numerous books and periodicals, including *Escape* and *Travel Holiday* magazines.

Brazilian photojournalist **Ricardo Beliel** works for news publications throughout the world. He is a 1991 winner of the Interpress photo award from the International Organization of Journalists.

Annie Griffiths Belt has shot many magazine and book projects for National Geographic. Her work has appeared in *Life, Smithsonian, Fortune,* and *American Photo,* and in such books as *A Day in the Life of Ireland* and *The Power to Heal.*

Jean-Claude Coutausse began his photojournalism career in the 1980s. His work has appeared in *Newsweek, Time, l'Express,* and *The New York Times.* He currently works for *Télérama, Le Monde, Libération,* and the French edition of *National Geographic.*

Michael Coyne's work has appeared in such magazines as *Newsweek, Life, Time, National Geographic, Sports Illustrated,* and *Vogue.* His numerous honors include awards from the National Press Photographers Association, Overseas Press Club of America, and the Australian government for service to photography.

Louis DeLuca is a staff photographer for the *Dallas Morning News* and a four-time winner of the National Press Photographers Association Regional Photographer of the Year.

Based in Portland, Oregon, **Mark Downey** was named Photographer of the Year by the Society of American Travel Writers in 2004 and is a two-time winner of the organization's gold award for culture and people photography. His work has been published in numerous books, magazines, and newspapers, including *Forbes, Islands, National Geographic, Geo, Newsweek, Time,* and *The New York Times.* He runs the Lucid Images photo agency, a library of more than 500,000 images documenting world cultures and the leaders and issues of our time. Downey won a Lowell Thomas Award for travel writing in 2004.

Paul Doyle is a freelance photographer based in London whose work focuses on travel and social issues.

Victor Englebert specializes in documenting the world's indigenous cultures. His pictures have been published in such magazines as *National Geographic, Smithsonian,* and *Natural History.*

Adventurer, mountain climber, and award-winning photographer **Olivier Föllmi** has produced several books, including *Buddhist Himalayas, Homage to the Himalayas,* and *India.*

Specializing in social issues, **Paul Fusco** has published widely in *Time, Life, Mother Jones,* and other magazines. His recent work includes projects on people living with AIDS in California, homelessness in New York, and the Zapatista uprising in Mexico.

A journalism professor at the University of New Mexico, **Miguel Gandert** has been photographing the people and landscapes of his native New Mexico for twenty years. His publications include the book *Nuevo México Profundo.*

Australian travel photographer **Jill Gocher** specializes in images of Asia, with an emphasis on Nepal and eastern Tibet.

A former staff photographer at *La Nación* in Argentina, **Russell Gordon** covers news, culture, and economic issues, including armed conflicts in Afghanistan, Cambodia, Yugoslavia, Burundi, and Mexico.

Louise Gubb covered South Africa's apartheid struggle and the advent of democracy under Nelson Mandela's presidency. Her images have been featured in two books on Mandela and have appeared in *Life, Time, Newsweek, Stern,* and *National Geographic.*

Robert Holmes, a two-time winner of the Travel Photographer of the Year award from the Society of American Travel Writers, has more than 30 books in print. His pictures have been featured in virtually every major travel publication.

Nominated for a Pulitzer Prize in 2004, **Chris Hondros** has documented conflicts in Kosovo, Sierra Leone, Afghanistan, Kashmir, the West Bank, Iraq, and Liberia. His work has appeared on the covers of *Newsweek, The Economist, Stern,* and other publications.

Stephen Huyler is an anthropologist, photographer, and writer specializing in the traditional cultures of India. His books include *Meeting God, Painted Prayers,* and *Village India.*

Named Travel Photographer of the Year by the Society of American Travel Writers in 2000, **Bob Krist** works regularly for such magazines as *National Geographic Traveler, Smithsonian,* and *Islands.* His books include *In Tuscany, Spirit of Place,* and *Down the Shore.*

Magnum photographer **Steve McCurry** has covered conflicts in Beirut, Cambodia, Yugoslavia, Afghanistan, the Gulf War, the Iran-Iraq War, and elsewhere. His images appear in a wide range of books and magazines and are often featured in *National Geographic.* Among his many honors is an unprecedented four first prizes in the World Press Photo Contest in 1984.

Wally McNamee produced more than a hundred cover photos during his 30-year career with *Newsweek* magazine. He has photographed every president from Dwight Eisenhower to George W. Bush and is a four-time winner of the White House News Photographers Association Photographer of the Year Award.

Abraham Menashe describes himself as a practitioner of humanistic photography, which "examines the full range of human emotions from a spiritual perspective." His many books include *The Face of Prayer, Inner Grace,* and *The Healing Moment.*

Javad Montazeri studied photography at Azad University in Tehran, Iran, and has worked for Reuters and other news agencies.

Photojournalist **Narinder Nanu** shoots for AFP news agency.

Richard Nowitz shoots for *National Geographic World,* and his work appears often in numerous other magazines, including *Time, Condé Nast Traveler,* and *Smithsonian.* He is the principal photographer of several Insight travel guides as well as gift books on Israel, Turkey, and Egypt. He was named Travel Photographer of the Year by the Society of American Travel Writers in 1996.

Christine Osborne is the proprietor of a stock photography agency specializing in travel and world religions.

Andrea Pistolesi specializes in ethnographic reportage. He works on assignment for magazines such as *Islands* and *Travel & Leisure,* and has produced books on Indonesia, Hinduism, and Eastern Christianity.

A National Geographic photographer for more than two decades, **Steve Raymer** teaches photojournalism at Indiana University. His books include *Land of the Ascending Dragon: Rediscovering Vietnam* and *Living Faith: Inside the Muslim World of Southeast Asia.* He was named Magazine Photographer of the Year by the National Press Photographers Association in 1976 and is a four-time winner of first-prize awards from the White House News Photographers Association.

Photojournalist **J. R. Ripper** covers social issues and political news in Brazil. His reports on land conflicts, indigenous people, and slave labor are used by various organizations to promote peace and social justice.

Swedish photographer and writer **Anders Ryman** has worked for publications throughout the world, including *Condé Nast Traveler, Geo, Islands,* and *National Geographic Nordic.*

Tom Salyer is an editorial photographer based in Miami, Florida.

Peter Sanders has been chronicling the Islamic world for more than twenty years. His pictures have appeared in *Time, The Observer, The Sunday Times Magazine, Paris Match,* and *Al Majalla.*

David Sanger was named 1998 Photographer of the Year by the Society of American Travel Writers. His work has been featured in magazines such as *National Geographic Traveler, Escape,* and *Sunset* as well as in calendars by UNICEF and the Sierra Club.

Israeli photojournalist **Uriel Sinai** was awarded first prize by World Press Photo for general news stories in 2005.

Raised in China and now residing in Seattle, photographer **Keren Su** is the founder of China Span stock photo agency.

Photographer and writer **Stephen Trimble** specializes in the people and natural history of the American West. His books include *The Sagebrush Ocean, Blessed By Light,* and *Our Voices, Our Land.* He is a recipient of the Sierra Club's Ansel Adams Award for photography and conservation.

Named 2003 Magazine Photographer of the Year by the National Press Photographers Association, **Ami Vitale** shoots for publications such as *Time, Newsweek,* and *U.S. News and World Report.*

Nevada Wier is a travel photographer whose work takes her to the far corners of the globe. Her images appear regularly in magazines such as *Geo, National Geographic Adventure, Outdoor Photographer,* and *Islands.* Her books include *Adventure Travel Photography* and *The Land of Nine Dragons.*

Alison Wright is a freelance photojournalist based in San Francisco, California, specializing in the people and cultures of the world's remote places. She is a 1993 recipient of the Dorothea Lange Award in documentary photography. Her books include *A Simple Monk, The Spirit of Tibet,* and *Faces of Hope.*

ACKNOWLEDGMENTS
Special thanks to kindred spirit Mark Downey for his encouragement during the long course of this project. Thanks also to Brett Trainor for his support, good humor, and generous spirit; Ingrid Lynch for design advice; Edward Jardim for editorial assistance; Bob Krist for good conversation and his great eye; and the staff of the Holland-Alexandria Public Library in New Jersey, who supplied me with many of the research materials for this book.
— John Gattuso